225
6R

THE PRIEST AND THE UNCONSCIOUS

THE PRIEST

AND

THE UNCONSCIOUS

BY

ERWIN RINGEL, M.D.
and
REV. DR. WENZEL VAN LUN

Edited and translated from the German
by
MEYRICK BOOTH, (Ph.D. Jena)

MCMLIV
THE NEWMAN PRESS,
WESTMINSTER, MARYLAND

First published in U.S.A. by The Newman Press,
Westminster, Maryland.

Published in Germany under the title Die Tiefenpsychologie hilft
dem Seelsorger by Verlag Herder Vienna.

Nihil Obstat: *Jacobus Bastible*
                    Censor Deputatus

Imprimatur: ✠*Cornelius*
                    Episcopus Corcagiensis

26th May, 1954

Printed in the Republic of Ireland
by The Kerryman Ltd., Russell St., Tralee

CONTENTS

CONTENTS

INTRODUCTION

IT HAS FOR LONG been the primary task of pastoral medicine to make priests acquainted with those aspects of medical knowledge necessary or useful in the care of souls. In more recent years, a second and no less important task has arisen: to introduce doctors to the problems of pastoral medicine; to make them aware of the advantages of a more universal outlook in their own science, one that can open the way to fresh discoveries and lift medicine out of the rut of a one-sided positivism. At the same time the primary work of pastoral medicine remains unaffected. As a borderland between two faculties it finds itself in much the same position as juridical medicine.

In the present study, Dr. Erwin Ringel, a doctor and psychologist, in collaboration with a theologian, Dr. van Lun, has undertaken to provide a scientific and empirically well-founded introduction to the psychology of the unconscious and its practical application. Their chief aim is to convince the priest that a certain knowledge in this field can give him invaluable aid just where *he most needs it*: namely, in regard to a number of cases usually the most difficult and the least rewarding. Before the days of modern psycho-therapy, these were the most troublesome and difficult for doctors also: we need only think of hysteria and neurosis, disorders dreaded by doctors, who could do little to help the sufferers, often regarded as the victims of imaginary complaints.

Yet, today, such cases are among the most worthwhile that a doctor can handle, thanks to the pioneer work of those who probed the depths of the soul and explored the world of the unconscious with its resistances, its riddles, and its dangerous abysses, thus rendering it *understandable* and open to curative influences. The priest, as much as the doctor, can now look upon these patients in quite a new light; and he has reason to be grateful to the authors of this little book if their tireless work has succeeded in opening up new paths, to the great benefit of those entrusted with the care of souls, at the same time indicating the great value of collaboration with doctors in this particular field of medicine.

This study undoubtedly fills a gap in the somewhat too prolific literature of psychoanalysis and the psychology of the unconscious in general. Let us hope that it may serve as a foundation for the future close co-operation of priest and doctor.

DR. ALBERT NIEDERMEYER,

Professor of Pastoral Medicine
at the University of Vienna.

Vienna, December, 1952.

CHAPTER I

THE PSYCHOLOGY OF THE UNCONSCIOUS AND THE PRIEST

ARCHBISHOP SHEEN OF NEW YORK has said that the modern man, in his quest for inner peace, prefers to begin with psychology rather than with Catholic metaphysics. We shall therefore begin with psychology.

The success of a priest in his practical work must depend largely upon his ability to establish good contacts with those entrusted to his care; the relationship between man and man plays a decisive role. It is absolutely essential to grasp the personality of the other, to enter into his conflicts and problems and to make it clear, in word and deed, that one sympathises. No two people are alike; even the same problem is experienced differently by each. If the priest is to discover the right approach, he must penetrate the mind of the individual. Even these few sentences must convince the reader that psychological questions are of great significance in the work of spiritual direction; and that, accordingly, an adequate knowledge of psychology is very valuable to a priest.

Originally, psychology confined itself to the conscious actions of men and women. But in the early days of the present century a considerable body of new knowledge was brought to light, which showed beyond doubt that the life of the soul was by no means confined to such actions; that other factors, of which we seem to be totally unconscious, are all the time active in our personalities. To give one everyday example: A may be, to all appearances, on the best of terms with B, and all his actions may support this view, but, in the depth of his heart, A may have no sympathy with B and may even hate him. Disagreeable impressions, experiences, sensations, feelings and wishes, from early childhood onwards, seem to be forgotten and to sink into oblivion. But in reality they are merely suppressed, and become part of the contents of the subconscious mind, whence some appropriate situation or opportunity causes them to manifest themselves in a symbolic form which is not understood by the conscious mind. This doctrine of suppression and the subconscious—sometimes called 'depth-psychology'—is not content with studying what happens on the surface, but delves to deeper causes. It has essentially enriched our knowledge and even if, as we shall see later, we have for good reasons to adopt a critical attitude towards this type of psychology, we must not fail to examine its discoveries with an earnest mind. In this, we should not allow ourselves to be repelled *a priori* by the fact that depth-psychology originated with men like Freud and Adler who stood quite outside our own life-outlook.

Both the psychology of the conscious and that of the subconscious are of immense importance to the priest. There is an ancient theological principle: *Gratia supponit naturam*—Grace builds on nature. This must not be wrongly interpreted. It does not mean that the work of grace is determined by the structure of the natural world. As faithful Catholics, we do not doubt for a moment that grace can accomplish anything and everything. But the priest, as an instrument of God upon earth, must do his best to remove anything that could make the operation of grace more difficult. If the natural psychological attitude of an individual is abnormal, this means, in practice, that the supernatural life is seriously endangered.

Many people today are psychologically ill. The symptoms of neurosis are widespread and steadily increasing. Consider some of the more conspicuous: anxieties and obsessions, supersensitivity, lack of confidence, abnormal irritability, depressions, drug and other addictions, sexual disturbances, and all those vague shifting physical complaints which have no organic explanation, because they are of psychic origin. Those who are affected by these symptoms suffer doubly because they do not know what is the matter.

The discoveries of Freud began with an investigation of these symptoms. He succeeded in tracing them back to past experiences which had been thrust down into the subconscious. This relationship was convincingly demonstrated by the fact that, when the experiences in question were brought up into the conscious mind, the symptoms disappeared.

Since the researches of Freud, some fifty years have elapsed during which a dynamic development of the psychology of the unconscious (depth-psychology) has taken place, a fact not easily accepted by a certain section of opinion which would prefer to put the clock back. Today, there are three leading schools of thought in the psychology of the unconscious: psycho-analysis of the Freudian type; the individual psychology of the Adler school; and the analytical psychology of C. G. Jung. Common to all three is the exploration of the unconscious mind. (In a sense, all these are branches of psycho-analysis, but the term is sometimes restricted to the Freudian school alone. Tr. Note). There is general agreement, also, on the fact that the most significant suppressions, in which psychic factors are thrust down into the unconscious, take place during early childhood; and, from all three sides, convincing scientific proof of this has been brought forward.

Differences begin to emerge, however, when we consider what constitutes the levels *below* consciousness. Freud assumed that the main elements consisted, first and foremost, of 'morally unacceptable things' which had been thrust down for the very reason that they were not acceptable. His entire system is directed towards digging out these 'things' and bringing them up into the light of the conscious mind. The unconscious is thus envisaged by Freud as *personal*; it is the result of the phenomenon of suppression, and its contents essentially comprise *instinctive* tendencies. Jung, on the other hand, sees the matter quite differently. He lays weight on his belief that subconscious processes, like others, form an integral part of the life of the organism as a whole, and therefore, as a matter of course, must participate in its dynamic development and instinctive life. He regards them, indeed, as, in a certain sense, *results* of the action of instinct. He denies that the psyche is to be regarded as composed of elements derived from the instinctive levels. It is to be perceived that Jung's system rests, to some extent, upon considerations connected with the theory of knowledge, and to a much greater extent upon philosophical ideas. Jung draws special attention to a quotation from Freud: 'An instinct can never be the object of consciousness; but the idea which represents it can be. In the unconscious, too, an instinct cannot be represented otherwise than by an idea.' Jung then asks: to whom is an instinct below the conscious level represented? He arrives at the conclusion that the unconscious cannot be in one place, and the conscious in another; and he stresses the unity of the psyche as a 'conscious-unconscious whole.' According to his view, the various psychic processes are arranged like a scale, the psyche is able to run up and down the range of consciousness. Now it approaches the instinctive activities; now it draws near to the other end, where the spirit leads, and is even able to assimilate the instinctive processes which are opposed to the spirit. The concept of the unconscious is not in Jung's case confined to instinctive tendencies. Jung goes beyond Freud in a formal sense when he perceives not only a *personal* unconscious but, in addition to this, what he calls the *collective unconscious*: a doctrine which can easily be understood in a pantheistic sense. He stresses the existence of a collective body of unconscious factors, characterised by a dim unconscious *a priori* knowledge and completely impersonal in their nature.

The individual psychology of Adler occupies a position mid-way between Freud and Jung. To Adler, everything is unconscious whose relationship to the whole personality we do not understand. (*Theory and Practice of Individual Psychology*). This school is not so much concerned with causal relationships; its outlook is towards the *end*; it seeks to understand the goal towards which the personality is directed. We are not able, says Adler, to think, to feel, to will, or to act, unless there is a goal present in the mind. The problem becomes one of finding out what these goals are; and, as a result of his researches in this field, he proved that, fundamentally speaking, the formative forces governing the life of an individual follow a consistent line; this he called the *Leitlinie*. Individual psychology, accordingly, sees the unconscious as the life-aim pursued by an individual, even though he may not be actually aware of that life-aim. Hence this school speaks of the 'real' and the 'secret' goal of life. This must not be regarded as merely the goal of particular actions, but as the ultimate goal of the individual's life; his 'way of living,' i.e., the manner in which he seeks to master his problems and difficulties. The explanation of the unconscious in the earlier Adlerian literature was inadequate; so much so that many critics assumed that the school did not recognise an unconscious. Recently, Ringel and W. Spiel have not only disarmed these critics, but have shown that the unconscious neurotic life-pattern, regarded from the standpoint of the Adlerian school, represents the very source of one's way of living. They emphasised, further, that individual psychology—like that of the Freudian school—understood the unconscious in a personal sense; but that, in contrast to Freud, the school of Adler held that *all* psychic tendencies (and not just those of an instinctive nature) can be found in the unconscious.

There are also other points in which the three schools we have mentioned differ vitally from one another. It is often somewhat depressing to perceive that the very men whose business it is to understand human nature from every angle, are able to understand everything—except the views of psychological schools opposed to their own. We cannot in this study give a complete account of the structure of the different systems; but we feel it necessary to draw the readers' attention to some of the more fundamental elements in the teachings of the three schools. In doing so we are, to some extent, indebted to the comprehensive studies of Federn-Meng, Paul Polak, and W. Toman. It will be understood that the difficult task of selection has been performed with a view to making this book useful for the priest.

It is especially difficult to make a selection in the case of the Freudian school with its immense literature. The most important element, in our view, is the psycho-analytical conception of the structure of personality. According to the Freudians, this structure is a functional unity consisting, basically, of three sections: the *ego*, in the narrower sense, which receives perceptions from outside as well as those from within—such as instinctive urges, wishes and tendencies—all in so far as they can get past the censorship. The latter, in its turn, is exercised by the second section, the *super-ego*. This rules over the desires and instinctive urges surging up from the unconscious and impelling us to action; and, acting from a social angle, it allows some of these to go by, while others are refused entry to the level of consciousness. Finally there is a third section existing in all of us: namely the realm of *unconscious instincts and desires*, embracing original primitive tendencies not adapted to social needs. This forms a kind of reservoir of chaotic, dynamic elements in personality: Freud calls this the *Id*.

The ego has a relative function, for it must attempt to establish harmony between the urges surging up from the unconscious, and the possibilities and obstacles connected with the outer world and the *super-ego*. According to this school, our actions derive from the co-operation of the above three sections of personality. Neurosis results from conflicts which break out between these sections. The *Id* is liable to create disturbances in which sexual and aggressive tendencies having their origin in childhood and now established as fixed elements, play a decisive part. The Freudian school has been extremely active in this field and great light has been thrown upon the emotional life of the young child, especially with regard to its early sexual stirrings. The old-fashioned view that sexuality begins with puberty is scientifically untenable. A childish sexuality does exist, but it differs completely from adult sexuality. The very first days in the child's life are of considerable significance in this connection. A little later comes the time when the child learns cleanliness (the *oral* and *anal* phases in Freudian language). Psychoanalysis has revealed the importance of sexual shocks or disturbances in these early days and has shown that the phase in which the shock is experienced is important. It has drawn attention to certain tendencies in the field of childish experience—for example, an inclination to the parent of the opposite sex—which are especially inclined to produce complexes (conflicts between conscious and unconscious wishes). There is the Oedipus Complex, for example, to which we shall return. On the other hand, disturbances of various kinds may result from a false development of the *super-ego*. The Freudian school especially emphasises the danger of a too strongly developed *super-ego* leading to an unnatural suppression of sexual wishes and hence to neurotic symptoms.

According to Alexander (F. Alexander and T. M. French: *Psychoanalytic Therapy*, N. York, 1946), psychoanalysis of this school distinguishes the following types of character:

1. The criminal type. Here the *super-ego* is weak, and the inhibiting tendencies which act as a brake with normal persons do not function; thus the lower tendencies, normally held in check, occupy the conscious mind and lead to criminal acts.

2. The neurotic, or instinctive, type. Here the instinctive uncensored impulses of the unconscious have a dominant influence, but the existence of moral inhibitions causes strong feelings of guilt. Disorder is present, first and foremost, within the *ego* itself which is not capable of bringing about a working balance between the two opposed tendencies, instinct and conscience. Alexander says that these types carry within themselves the criminal and the judge.

3. The inhibited type. Here the *super-ego* is excessively developed,

making the individual shy, full of fears, and often unable to pursue any line of conduct wholeheartedly.

4. The healthy type. Here the three sections work together in harmony, creating a well-balanced personality.

Seen from the Freudian angle, every psychic urge or wish is, in the last analysis, fed by the stream of the sexual instinct. This basic urge is called by Freud the *libido*. To him, the relationship between instinct and personality is more important than the strength of the urge itself. The aim of psychoanalytical treatment on Freudian lines is to put the patient in such a position that he can transfer the *libido* from a lower to a higher level, turning its energy towards social goals. Freud called this elevation of sexual energy *sublimation*.

While this school placed the *Id* in the forefront, the *ego* playing a secondary role, in the individual school (Adler) the main weight is transferred from the *Id* to the *ego*, thus emphasising the responsible personal element. Man is seen as a unified whole, an entity with a purpose. This is indicated by the 'final' mode of regarding life —to which reference has been made. Man is not pushed; he either seeks a goal, or is drawn along by it. With the school of Adler, the basic human experience is a feeling of inferiority, derived either from the subordinate position occupied by children in relation to adults, or from a real or perhaps imaginary organic defect (organic inferiority). This may lead to a pathological inferiority complex, or it may not: the decisive factor is the manner in which the experience is dealt with inwardly. In the case of a neurotic development the experience is not mastered; the feeling of inferiority is retained, festers inwardly and in times of difficulty it will manifest itself, causing discouragement. As a general rule, this feeling of inferiority is over-compensated. The subject seeks to overcome it to an exaggerated extent by a more or less pathological self-assertion, which, in extreme cases, shows itself in a desire to be godlike. The relationship between the feeling of inferiority and the urge towards self-assertion is one of polarity. The degree of development of the one depends upon that of the other, because they are in fact different sides of the same thing—the neurosis itself. The urge to self-assertion may lead to anti-social actions, causing the subject to turn away from the community to which, by reason of his inward nature, he naturally belongs. According to the teaching of the individual school of psychology, the individual cannot be thought of except in relationship to the community. In the early publications of this school we perceive the danger of a failure to progress beyond the limits of a mere 'social morality.' However, later works by O. Spiel and Ringel enlarged this concept by assigning weight to the fact that man is able to *value*, and that a general validity is attributed to the values set up; they do not refer to social laws, which vary from place to place and time to time. But, through his neurosis, he places himself outside the community; he becomes ego-centric instead of being socio-centric. Of decisive importance is the objective achievement which a man is able to accomplish, in the course of his life, through his mastery of the central tasks of life: love, family, profession or occupation.

The 'complex psychology' of Jung is largely built upon the assumption of a collective unconscious, and a large part of his work is concerned with this. He believes in the existence of forces which have become unconscious, not through being thrust down into the depths during the life-time of the individual, but by virtue of a phylogenetic process. They are part of the inheritance of the race. In the same manner, the father and mother ideas of an individual are based not only upon his personal experiences, but also upon collective primordial ideas of man and woman (*animus* and *anima*) handed down from the remote past. These ancient original concepts are called *archetypes* by Jung. Other archetypal ideas are, for example, such primitive components of consciousness as danger, birth, death, light and dark. These archetypes are associated with specific urges impelling towards action.

In order to support his views, Jung occupies himself with the interpretation of numerous ancient myths. Mingled with the purely psychological, his work contains many elements of a philosophical and mythological nature. Jung deals by preference, both in his theoretical and practical work, with men and women in the second half of their lives. He attributes a special significance to the summit of the curve of life—the high noon of life—and speaks of a turning point which seems able to bring about fundamental transformations in the life of the individual. He emphasizes the dynamic evolution of a human life, the course it runs, directed towards a specific goal. The curve of life may be compared to the curve described by a bullet; leaving a position of rest it soars upwards to reach the summit of its flight and then descends to another position of rest. A main cause of neurotic trouble in later life is, according to Jung, the unwillingness of a man or woman to co-operate psychologically with nature in describing the sinking curve. The lack of harmony between the individual and the curve which is his destiny, sometimes manifests itself during the period of ascent. The bullet soars upwards in a biological sense, Jung explains, but, psychologically, it hangs back. The individual lags behind his age; he clings to childhood, as if the bullet did not want to trace its curve. He holds back the hands of the clock and would like to think time stands still. When the descending period begins, such states are more strongly manifested, for now the fear of death—dimly felt in earlier days—looms large and grim. This is the time of the birth of death; and, as Jung urges, the only man who can preserve his psychic health is the one who is ready to accept this fact. 'The soul is nourished through the life of nature. He who will not co-operate in this life remains suspended in mid-air; he becomes numb. For this reason, so many men and women wither up when they grow old. They look back longingly to the past, their hearts filled with a secret fear of death. They withdraw from the life-process—at least psychologically—and remain fixed in the past, feeding on memories of youth, and having no living relationship to the present.'

The priest will do well to pay particular attention to these views of Jung, for he, more than other men, deals with the problem of the fear of death. (We need hardly draw attention to the fact that this is not the only aspect of the care of souls in the case of aging persons: in particular, we have the possibility of senile dementia in more or less severe forms. The problems thus arising go beyond the scope of this study). They acquire an added importance from the fact that the other schools of depth-psychology have neglected to assign to this problem the attention it deserved. O. Kauders (*Nervenarzt*: 7/6 1934), writing from the standpoint of psychiatry, made valuable additions to our knowledge in this field.

*   *   *   *   *

Psychotherapy is the name given to the practical application of the psychology of the unconscious (or depth-psychology) in the treatment of disorders. The significance of this method lies in the fact that, by means of repeated verbal exchanges between the psychotherapeutic doctor and the patient, the material buried in the subconscious mind is called back into consciousness, thereby removing the disordered psychic states. The different systems have their own methods of working along these lines. In each case, much resistance has to be overcome because the patient desires, unconsciously, to hold fast to the symptoms; the method must take this into account and develop a strategy for overcoming this difficulty. Especially noteworthy is the technique of 'free association' worked out by Freud: the patient is called upon to relate all the ideas which come to his mind in relation to an event, object, or dream. This method makes possible a kind of unrolling of the contents of the lower subconscious levels, and thus offers important therapeutic advantages. We should, however, point out certain possible dangers attaching to this technique, more especially if it be carried out by persons not possessing the necessary respect for human personality and, possibly, over-valuing the significance of sexual elements. Pius the Twelfth has pointed this out in impressive words: 'In truth, one cannot consider morally permissible, without due consideration, the bringing up to the level of consciousness all the representations, emotions and sexual experiences, which lie dormant in the memory and the unconscious, thereby reactivating them. If the protests arising from a sense of human and Christian dignity are heeded, who would risk making the claim that this manner of treatment does not carry with it any moral danger, either immediate or future, when, even if the therapeutic necessity of unlimited exploration be affirmed, this necessity is not, after all, established?' Apart from this, each of the three above-mentioned schools has its own therapeutic purpose and its own mode of thought and approach.

Life can be looked upon as *action*, as *experience*, and as a *task*. Each of these three approaches is related to one of the three systems. The individual school regards life as purposeful action. The Freudians regard life as experience—the question being asked: what have you allowed yourself to experience and what have you rejected? Where is the filter in your mind which admits certain elements, and those alone, to reach you and become experiences? Jung, on the other hand, sees life as a task and enquires into its meaning. The aims of the therapeutic methods are defined according to these different outlooks. These have been formulated by the psychologist, F. Birnbaum in this manner: individual psychology demands that the former purpose should be replaced by a new one ; the Freudians call for the examination of the suppressed elements held back by the censorship, and aim at freedom and the removal of anxiety; while the school of Jung attaches a high value to joy and suffering as components of human life and demands that the meaning of life be understood through the positive acceptance of both elements. V. Frankl (*Arztliche Seelsorge*: Deuticke, Vienna, 1946) puts forward similar views, using the language of existential philosophy and holding that neurosis is conditioned by 'existential conflicts,' by 'spiritual necessity.' The views of Frankl form a valuable addition to our psychological knowledge, especially as regards his emphasis upon the spiritual aspect and his indication of the possibility of controlling instincts (although individual psychology had already taught the latter); all the same, these views must not be made the occasion of devaluing, or even over-looking, the basic new discoveries of the three great schools of depth-psychology. If we are to obtain a complete picture of the human being, we must examine him from below as well as from above. It is sufficiently obvious that a religious man will hardly succumb to an idea which places a one-sided emphasis upon the life of instinct. Even more dangerous, however, can be one-sided emphasis upon the spiritual life, a fact made clear by Caruso in the following terms: 'Many neurotic complexes lead to a characteristically impatient exaggerated spiritualised attitude; and indications of this attitude can be found in modern psychology also. Thus the gnostic tendency in Jung's psychology is inclined to represent self-realisation and the salvation of self in the spirit as achieved through pure knowledge. Other tendencies in depth-psychology (until recently popular), undervalue seriously the instinctive aspect of personality. Such tendencies may be understood very well as a reaction against the materialism of Freud but I perceive in them dangers greater than those attached to the orthodox Freudian school. They are exactly suited to lead idealistically minded people astray, by means of an exaggerated spirituality interpreted along Manichean lines. Moreover, through strengthening of the ego to the point of blinding it to reality, they act in a manner hostile to the true integration of the necessary relationship between self and others. They impart an absolute character to the relative in humanity, no matter how exalted this relative may seem to be.' In other words, it may now be said that through the exploration of the neuroses, depth-psychology has given us in a scientific way, the same picture of humanity as that shown so long ago by the Christian revelation. Man stands in between angel and animal

—between spirit and instinct. Any kind of one-sided view must destroy this picture. Today, the priest needs, more than ever, true insight into the essential nature of man: he must not be guided by illusions.

Thus we see that the three schools of thought represent three essential concepts— which are also of vital importance to spiritual directors—namely: action (individual psychology), passion (Jung), and liberation (Freud). Each of these is important, but the task of psychotherapy demands the co-operation of all three. For this reason, we should in the future earnestly pursue this more comprehensive approach—spoken of by Birnbaum as the 'convergence of the schools of depth-psychology,' and referred to by Niedermeyer as 'universal psychotherapy.'

That a knowledge of the psychology of the unconscious is of great value to priests cannot be doubted. If modern psychology has not been utilised in the work of the clergy to the extent that its real importance justifies, we cannot be altogether surprised. For, in spite of the deeply significant aid which it is able to render to those who have the care of souls, priests, up to now, have not received any adequate training in its methods; while a number of vague and highly misleading impressions have had considerable vogue. Many oppose the so-called 'new psychology' on principle; while others are convinced that it is identical with Freudian ideas —of which they know only that they originate from a materialistically minded scientist and unduly stress sexual matters. Others, again, equate Freud's philosophical ideas with his psychological work, believing that the two are indissolubly linked. Not a few priests and others have been prejudiced also by a belief that psychoanalysis aims at converting guilt into illness, thereby cancelling moral responsibility. Finally we find the view that the psychotherapist seeks to make himself the priest of our times, replacing and thrusting aside the real priests.

But, despite all doubts and difficulties, there is a steady increase in the interest priests are taking in 'depth-psychology.' They want to have clear ideas on the subject and it is urgently necessary that these should be imparted. For this reason the two authors of this study gave, in connection with the Catholic Academy, a course of lectures on the theme: 'The Importance of Depth-Psychology for the Practical Care of Souls.' The large attendance, and the keen and open-minded interest shown by the clergy, were responsible for the publication of this little book, which contains the lectures already given. In the future the material will be revised, improved and extended. This study is offered in the hope that a wider circle of priests will find it useful.

We propose to deal more especially with the following burning questions: Is the prejudice against the psychology of the unconscious justified? What should be the attitude of the priest towards this psychology in general, and towards the various schools of thought in particular? Should he make use of modern psychological methods? Should he work together with the doctor, and what form should this co-operation take? To what extent can psychic disorders influence the life of faith? How is the priest to know when a failure of religious life is due to neurosis? What should be his attitude towards a neurotic, and how can he judge him? And, finally, we wish to give some brief indications of the right approach to some special problems which may confront the priest, in dealing with certain awkward cases. We must be fully conscious of our duty to bring the Word of God to *all* men. We must never entertain the idea that in this or that case it is 'no good.' In this work a knowledge of analytical psychology can furnish valuable aid.

In the care of souls, we can employ not only the means provided by faith; but also those offered us by nature. If the man of today, as Bishop Fulton Sheen says (*Peace of Soul,* 1952), wishes to occupy himself more especially with psychological problems, even in the field of religion, this seems to indicate that the priest, too, should devote the most serious attention to this theme. In our view, however, the priest should do so as a matter of duty, apart from the spirit of the age. It is not because the psychology of the unconscious is 'modern,' and its problems widely discussed, that it is important to the priest, but because it is at *all* times his duty to keep in mind the life of nature and the foundations of psychic health. This is no question of a passing fashion, or of some special demand peculiar to the present day, but of a deep necessity independent of time; for the priest lives for both time and eternity, for nature and for what is above nature. We are supported in our plea by Dr. Donceel S. J., Professor at the Fordham University, New York, who says: 'Even if we never make use ourselves of the methods of modern analytical psychology, the increased depth of insight into human nature which they will bring to us will enable us to understand those who look to us to help them.'

The psychologists of the unconscious can proudly point to the fact that they have brought about a real revolution in the field of medicine. In place of the one-sided, materialistic and somatic conception of man, formerly so dominant, they have clearly emphasised the importance of the moral and spiritual elements, placing them in the forefront of the picture. They have done much to transcend the differences between science and religion. It should now be the task of the representatives of both to translate this theoretical reconciliation into practice. We trust that this study—the result of the co-operation of a priest and a doctor—will promote this aim.

CHAPTER II.

THE ATTITUDE OF THE PRIEST

IN OUR TIME, the priest finds himself confronted with problems which, as he soon discovers, are beyond his power to solve. True, there have always been problems of this kind, when the priest knew that he was dealing with psychopathic individuals: for example, kleptomaniacs. Now, however, these difficulties have increased beyond measure. To name one or two examples only which are increasingly met with in the Confessional: we have self-abuse in young people; self-abuse in married life; and the failure to practise love of the neighbour. People tell us that they simply cannot get on with their relations and those around them. The result is family quarrels, marriage difficulties, etc. We talk to them and give them good advice, yet unfortunately we see that, in the end, these people turn against the Church, neglect their duties, and fail in their spiritual life.

In the case of those who still remain within the Church, receive the sacraments, and call themselves Catholics, there are two attitudes, to be noted. The first attitude casts all the blame on others; it is always the other fellow who is responsible for being hated, or it is the over-strong instinct that is to blame if one does not live chastely. The second attitude is to take all the blame to one-self, admitting freely that one is sinful—and then adding: 'I am really at the end of my powers, I can see nothing but an abyss opening at my feet. Through my frequent relapses—for example in the case of the sixth commandment—my will is so enfeebled that I give way to every temptation.'

An attempt can be made to overcome these failings through training and practice. But we are forced to acknowledge that, unfortunately, this is frequently not successful. A little knowledge of the psychology of the unconscious makes it clear why this is the case. A part of these failings is conditioned by the special mechanism of neurotic states, and thus cannot be overcome until the basic causes—of which the faulty conduct is an outward manifestation—are removed. Even if, by means of discipline and training, we can succeed in removing a neurotic symptom, while the neurosis itself remains, the latter will manifest itself again in some way which we are not able to anticipate: for example in the collapse of a marriage.

We will not go so far as to say that neurotic tendencies may not disappear for good, under the influence of a good priest who has no knowledge of modern psychology but who can exercise a healthy and sane influence over others. The same result might be achieved through the influence of a really sound community. But such cases are increasingly rare, as we may perceive from the enormous growth in the number of those who fall away from religious faith, particularly amongst the young. It is therefore to be desired that the priest should pay more attention than in the past to the natural psychic disposition of his penitent. We must warn him against an extreme supernaturalism ignoring natural forces and values. We would support the views of Rudin who has hit the nail truly on the head: 'Again and again the practical psycho-therapist receives the impression that many priests do not possess even a minimum of understanding for the gifts bestowed by nature, for the instinctive life given man by the will of God. Consequently, on the one hand, repressions on a grand scale are encouraged in a manner that is altogether naive, while all sorts of mental and spiritual inhibitions—even to the point of the paralysis and petrifaction of emotional life—are looked upon as "progress"; on the other hand, it happens too often that the urge towards satisfaction of a magical-mystical nature is actually promoted,

hus providing the right soil for the growth of unhealthy and
dangerous states of mind.'

It is accordingly clear that the priest of today must be in a
position to recognise neurosis when he comes across it. He must
be able to distinguish this psychic disorder from true insanity
(psychosis): this is usually possible because the neurotic case is
mentally intact and realises quite well how absurd his actions or
notions are, while the insane patient does not. For example, a
neurotic will say: 'I can't help constantly thinking all sorts of
indecent things about God; although I know this is nonsense,
I can't help doing it.' But a victim of insanity will say: 'I feel
that my neighbour is persecuting me,' and when the doctor says:
'Are you sure you do not imagine that?' he will answer: 'Oh no
—I know it for an absolute fact!' At the same time, cases can
arise where it is difficult to draw the line; finally, it should always
be the specialist in psychiatry who makes the actual diagnosis.
But the priest should be able to form at least a rough idea of
the position. Furthermore, the priest should be able to distinguish
between a definite case of obsessional neurosis and a case where
there are neurotic tendencies (common to nearly all of us!). As
we shall see later, this distinction is very important on moral-
theological grounds—a point especially emphasised by Brenninkmeyer. The obsessional neuroses are to be distinguished by typical
compulsory irrational mechanistic patterns of behaviour, repeating
themselves again and again, occurring in various fields of life
and recognised by the patient as being absurd and irrational; the
neurotic tendencies may be troublesome and inhibitive at this
or that point, and thus a source of failure or breakdown; but
they do not assume a compulsory character. Here again the priest
must rely upon the judgment of the responsible medical specialist;
but he will, of course, retain the right to pass a final moral
judgment.

The decision that the priest should send his neurotic penitents
to a psychotherapeutic specialist cannot be carried out without

new difficulties arising; since many priests, not always withou
reason, feel a horror of certain types of therapy and therapeutists

This brings us face to face with the problem of Sigmund Freud
his school of psychoanalysis, and its relation to moral and religiou
questions. For it is a regrettable fact that the distinguished Viennes
therapist did not remain strictly within the bounds of analysi
and therapy, but invaded the field of philosophy. It is unfortunat
that he made use of his analytical work to undertake an 'explanation
of religion. In his work, *The Future of an Illusion*, we read as follows
'In like manner, man does not personify the forces of natur
as simple human beings on a level with himself. This woul
not do justice to the overwhelming impression these forces mak
upon him. He sees them as father-symbols, and regards them a
gods. He thus follows a pattern which is not only infantile, but
as I have attempted to show, psycho-genetic. With the passag
of time, the first observations of the rule of law in nature wer
made, so that the forces of nature lost their human aspect. Bu
the helplessness of man remained and with it his yearning for
father and for gods. The gods retain their threefold task: to banisl
the terrors of nature; to reconcile man with the cruelties of fate
especially with the inevitability of death; and to provide com-
pensation for the sufferings and deprivations imposed upon him
by his life in a civilised community.'

Freud's outlook on life is sufficiently indicated by these words,
so that we can spare ourselves his views upon sacrifice and the
Eucharist. Du Boeuff and Kuiper are entirely right in their
statements that not a single religion—not even a pagan religion—
could be explained on these lines. Man is biologically fitted for
self-dependence and independence. He would bow to the power of
unalterable natural forces, but he would not make them into gods,
and under no circumstances would he bind himself to a god or
gods.

It must be admitted that Freud rendered poor service to the
cause of psychoanalysis when he dragged in his views upon

eligion and philosophy. Yet it would be a mistake, on account of these views, wholly to reject the analysis and therapy of Freud and his disciples. For, in the first place, his psychology of the unconscious is not a product of his life-outlook; rather is his outlook the product of his psychology. And, secondly, both Freud and his followers separate analysis and therapy, on the one hand, from philosophy, on the other. Today, the majority, even of the orthodox Freudian school, contend that questions of a philosophical and religious nature should be considered as irrelevant to the task of analysis. Even Freud himself, appears to have been basically of the same opinion, for he said: 'In reality psycho-analysis is a method of research, an instrument taking neither one side nor the other, like the infinitesimal calculus.' At the same time, it is sufficiently obvious that the question of life-outlook cannot be banished from the field of psychotherapy; for this reason the choice of the psychologist is a most responsible matter. A great deal must depend upon the view of human personality held by the psychotherapist. Today, more than ever, a return to the Thomistic outlook should be insisted upon, not only in respect of those practising psychotherapy but for all doctors. Otherwise they will never be able to grasp the immensely important psycho-somatic relationships which have to be taken into account if any really effective medical treatment is to become possible.

In this separation between therapy and philosophy of life, Jung differs from Freud. Jung looks upon all religions as of equal value and as coming under the head of psychological experiences and results, to be made use of in analysis on account of their value. In Jung's case, therefore, the psychotherapeutist appears to be a sort of priest, charged with proclaiming religious truths in which he does not believe. We will not speak of other systems, but it should be noted, in general, that one cannot perform a useful service to any religion by means of proofs of the existence of God based on unsuitable grounds—having as little cogency, in fact, as the so-called mathematical proof of God's existence.

The intention may be good, but the reasoning is not sound. He who proves too much proves nothing.

We have seen that it would be a mistake totally to reject psycho-analysis on account of Freud's views about life and philosophy. We will now turn to a consideration of Freud's analytical method, with particular reference to the point upon which it is usually attacked: its pan-sexuality. It should be made clear at the start that this pan-sexuality, if it be understood in the sense that the sex instinct is the only basic instinct, cannot fairly be attributed to Freud and his school, for he recognises other instincts. Nevertheless, we do find a tremendous over-valuation of the sexual element in Freud's case; for we are driven to conclude that he regards all the other instincts as deriving their power, in the last resort, from the *libido* (used by this school in the sense of psycho-sexual energy Tr. Note). This method of regarding the problem is not without its good side. Up to the time of Freud and even later—in some cases up to the present day—the human being was looked upon as a conglomeration of all sorts of instincts. Human conduct was accordingly looked upon as nothing more than the result of a combination of impulses derived from this assortment of instincts. Freud must be credited with the attempt to re-introduce a unified outlook on personality. His own philosophy and outlook prevented him from pressing forward to the point at which he could have discovered the Aristotelian concept of entelechy, which embodies the spiritual principle in man. A further mistake on his part was to view the *libido* as the primary human instinct. In our view the sexual urge is certainly not the primary instinct—not even if regarded solely as the instinct for the preservation of the species. But Freud maintained that the *libido* was primary, not only for the *Id* but also for the two other layers of personality the *ego* and the *super-ego*. Freud considered these three 'layers' as merging gradually into one another.

This view of the structure of personality, as layers of instinctive ife, naturally demands that the instincts, which are dynamic, must

ndergo a release, whenever the instinctive impulse reaches a given
oint of intensity. Such a conclusion is the logical consequence of
he manner in which Freudian analysis interprets the structure
f human personality. This is *in complete contradiction to the
aching of the Church, according to which the soul as forma corporis
etermines the whole man, including his instinctive life. It would be
ut of the question for a Catholic analyst to accept such consequences
s the above.* It is thus clear that the materialistic philosophy of
fe plays a part in the Freudian system, a fact sharply criticised
y Allers (*The Successful Error*, Washington, 1951). If, however,
ur starting point is the Aristotelian-Thomistic school, the above
sycho-analytical viewpoint should *not* be completely rejected.
or this school does not neglect the life of instinct; on the contrary,
assigns to it a field of its own. This is clear from the principle:
Passio antecedens minuit libertatem (antecedent passion diminishes
reedom). If we accept the importance of instinct in this sense we
ave to allow for the possibility that a situation of conflict can
rise, as a result of thwarting the release of instincts, and thus a
eurosis can develop. It is a fact that we do actually find situations
n which the sexual element is strongly present, and neuroses owe
heir origin to sexual conflicts. In view of the foregoing and of
he large amount of material collected by Freud, throwing abundant
ght upon this type of case, we are compelled to admit that
ven analytical psychologists who—like the author of this work—
lo not belong to the Freudian school, will certainly pay serious
ttention to the Freudian point of view in many cases. But
his sort of treatment must not on any account proceed on such
ines that the patient's conflicts are solved by a mere surrender
o instinct. This could have only one result: a definite worsening
f the neurotic condition. The success of an analysis lies in bringing
ack buried elements into the conscious mind, with consequent
lisappearance of the symptoms. Another valuable factor in
nalysis is 'transference.' (By 'transference' we understand that
he patient transfers to another person, at a later date, the feelings

he had towards his parents when a child. This operates strongly in the case of a neurotic and the analyst (psychotherapist) becomes a special object of this transference). 'The infantile situation is experienced over again, with the analyst as object. The success of a therapeutic treatment is essentially dependent upon a right employment of transference: on the one hand, the treatment cannot be carried out without the transference, but, on the other hand, it should not go too far and should be broken off at the right moment—otherwise the independence of the patient will fail to be established and the neurosis will be in fact strengthened. It must be noted at this point that it is, of course, possible that the priest will become the object of the transference. He must always bear this in mind and in more difficult cases—especially if he is not experienced—he should avoid critical situations by handing over to another priest in good time.

The view is often put forward that psychoanalysis, and in particular that aspect of it which deals with instinct, is bound up, of necessity, with a deterministic view of human personality, and thus tends to destroy freedom. In the same connection, it is asked if it does not represent all consciousness of guilt as being a form of illness? And as a matter of fact, when we think logically and consistently about the Freudian type of analysis, we might well come to the conclusion that there is no problem of responsibility. On the other hand, we who take our stand on Catholic principles do not deny that, in many cases, guilt and illness are so closely linked together that responsibility is lessened or even entirely abolished. But as soon as we place the principle of entelechy in the personality itself, and cease to regard it as rooted in any instinct, we have proclaimed the principle of human freedom.

In this connection we may point to the words of Alfred Adler, the founder of individual psychology: 'It is not so much a question of what an individual brings *with* him, as of the use he makes of what he brought.' This saying was recently enlarged upon by Oscar Spiel, who said: 'If the decisive factor which makes something out of what was brought, is the ego of a human being, then the bodily and environmental experiences of the individual can no longer be regarded as determined, in a necessary sense, but assume the character of forces, possibly temptations, operating from outside the ego. What is really determined is unavoidable, but the opportunities, or temptations, coming from without can be met either with a "Yes" or a "No".'

Here we note a difference, in principle, as compared with what we saw in the case of Freud. The latter saw everything as bound up with the libido, the instinctive, while, Adler gave its true value to the principle of entelechy, by placing it within the personality itself. Following up the teaching of Adler, we see that the instincts have value in as far as they are functions of organs, and then only. If, in the case of an individual, we find that an instinct is more strongly developed than would thus be accounted for, we are compelled to assume—in the absence of any organic disease—that the person in question makes *use* of this instinct in the pursuit of personal aims. This indicates that the Adlerian school, even more than scholastic philosophy, stresses personal freedom and responsibility. The significance of the 'more' lies in the fact that *passiones antecedentes* (to which we have referred above) cannot eliminate freedom and responsibility, except in cases of organic disease. The importance of the progress achieved by Adler as compared with Freud was made clear by Pope Pius XII in his well-known speech to the Congress of psychotherapists in Rome in April, 1953, when he said: 'The existence of each psychic faculty and function is justified by the end of the whole. What constitutes man is principally the soul, the substantial form of his nature. From it, ultimately, flows all human life. In the soul are rooted all the psychic dynamisms with their own structure and their organic laws. It is the soul which nature charges with the regulation of all energies, in so far as these have not yet reached their final determination.

'Given this ontological and psychic fact, it follows that it would be a departure from reality to attempt, in theory or in practice, to entrust the determining rôle of the whole to one particular factor, for example, to one of the elementary psychic dynamisms, and thus install a secondary power at the helm. Those psychic dynamisms may be *in* the soul, *in* man. They are not, however, the soul nor the man. They are energies of considerable intensity possibly, but nature has entrusted their direction to the central point, to the spiritual soul endowed with intelligence and will, which is normally capable of governing these energies. That these energies may exercise pressure upon one kind of activity does of another not necessarily signify that they determine it. It would be denying an ontological and psychical reality to question the soul's central place.'

The above cited Adlerian factors can, moreover, give the priest, in particular, valuable indications for his work. We must remember that in cases of sexual disturbances the personality as a whole is brought into disorder and makes use of sexuality for false purposes of its own. It is an unfortunate fact that many priests are themselves guilty of a species of 'pan-sexualism,' in as far as they look upon every kind of sexual disturbance as conditioned solely by instinctive forces: thus, for example, self-abuse is often branded as simply weakness in face of the sex instinct, and the exhortations of the priest take the form, 'You must be stronger in resisting this instinct; you must overcome it.' Such an attitude is certainly necessary in many cases; but often it does not go to the root of the matter, since—to take an example—self-abuse may be a symptom of a protest against the family and in this form it has relatively little to do with the sexual instinct. The overcoming of the habit in such a case will not take place until the attitude to the family has been changed.

While thus making the responsibility of the individual perfectly clear, we must remember that if responsibility be multiplied indefinitely, we must become the victims of an unhealthy pessimism. It is clear that a wrong attitude towards life can result from the lack of proper education in early years. This attitude will naturally be affected by further circumstances, such as the position of a child, as an only child, the last child in a family, or a child 'dethroned' by others; or the state of family life in the home, the presence of organic troubles in the child, etc. In addressing Catholics, we do not need to point out that, in the case of young children, there can be no such thing as 'guilt,' since the child is not old enough to carry responsibility. Moreover, the beginning of a neurosis (and it *does* begin in childhood) can be the cause of actions carried out under an inner compulsion. It must not be understood, however, that, henceforward, every action is free from guilt. It will be generally realised, to take an example, that in the case of a spiritless neurotic child, self-abuse will seem to offer a peculiarly suitable means of producing a feeling of superiority. This is not to say that, when a child begins to practise self-abuse, there is in all cases no guilt. If the habit is not an integral part of the child's neurotic system it does not as yet possess a compulsory character; it is an act of free will and thus a sinful act. Accordingly, at least the first acts must be looked upon as a capitulation of the free will, and we cannot attribute to them a character of compulsion *unless* such a character was acquired in early childhood before the beginnings of responsibility. It is from this standpoint that we must form a moral judgment in respect of these practices. Yet the standpoint of the therapeutist cannot be the same. Since it is a question of a negative experience, he will certainly attach a high degree of importance to these practices. If he says that self-abuse is of no special significance, he does not intend this as a *moral* judgment; he speaks solely as an analyst, and what he seeks to convey is that the neurosis is the primary thing and the sin or fault is, from the standpoint of psycho-analysis, no more than a symptom of the illness. But we must bear in mind that the therapeutist is not a priest who must express a judgment on moral problems; he is a doctor and his sole concern is with the illness which he seeks to cure. (We shall return to this topic in the next chapter). Rümke and many others assert that self-abuse is normal and a healthy sign. Such a view must be decisively rejected. But, on the other hand, we should not assert that the habit, begun as a free act, must always remain a free act; in other words, that a neurotic bears the whole responsibility. If the self-abuse of a neurotic is unconsciously made a part of his life pattern, then it acquires in the case of a genuine obsessional neurosis, the character of a compulsion. From the standpoint of psychoanalysis, it should be added that the habit of self-abuse is always accompanied by feelings of guilt, and it would be a mistake, from the analyst's standpoint, to do anything to add to these feelings. Neurotic subjects are found who assert that they can manage their lives with the aid of religion alone, and yet find it impossible to get rid of these habits. From the therapeutic standpoint this cannot be done until the neurosis has been cured. And if, as a result of training and discipline, a point is reached when self-abuse is no longer practised, this may have little therapeutic value. In not a few cases, the reaction is actually *unfavourable*, because the neurotic pattern becomes more rigid. The problem is to break up the neurosis itself, and restore *freedom of will* to the sufferer. (Later we shall discuss the methods employed). It must be our aim to clear the way for the patient to recover his full responsibility for action.

Thus, seen in the light of analytical psychology, much that would appear as guilt when envisaged objectively, is in fact illness, and does not involve subjective guilt. We must therefore look upon the objectively sinful actions of the neurotic subject, in so far as they form part of his compulsory pattern conditioned by disease, as *peccata materialia* (material sins) which have not become *peccata formalia* (formal sins). The therapeutist is not concerned with this moral judgment, but, through his treatment, he can bring the patient to a point where his actions become those of a free agent. These actions are no longer subject to a morbid compulsion, but assume the form of temptations offered to the free will (Oscar Spiel). He is free to perform or not perform the actions thus presenting themselves to his mind. If he then chooses to perform them, they come under the head of formal sins. In the light of the foregoing, we cannot accept the charge that analytical psychology regards all sins as if they were forms of disease. Quite the reverse; it is precisely the psychotherapeutist who seeks to banish the element of slavish addiction, the compulsory patterns of neurosis, and to establish the free decision of the human spirit. This process of banishment and liberation is not performed over-night; it requires practice, and involves decision, relapse, renewed decision. From a moral standpoint, we may regard it as a *consuetudo retractata* (a habit that has been given up). For now we can speak truly of a habit being given up, since the patient, or the penitent as the case may be, has taken the only possible step by which he can get rid of his bad habits—namely psychotherapeutic treatment. As long as the neurosis lasts we cannot speak with accuracy of a *consuetudo retractata*, because the patient—even if with his *conscious* mind he desires not to sin—subconsciously intends to continue the bad habits. It should be added that it would not be correct to place every sinful act of a neurotic under the head of illness. A psychiatrist, when asked for a statement with regard to a punishable offence, must ask himself not only if the person in question is in a general sense responsible or not, but also—and more especially—what is the relation between the type of illness and the type of offence: in other words, is there a specific connection between the offence and the psychic illness of the person charged? Does the act belong to the pattern of the illness, so that it could justly be described as taking place under a neurotic compulsion? In like manner, when passing moral judgment upon the acts of a neurotic patient, we have to ask if his conduct fits, of necessity, into the pattern of his abnormality? In the case of a real compulsory neurosis, we can assume the diseased nature of *all* the acts of the patient; *in so far* as they are subject to compulsion. We have in mind the theories of Künkel (*Einführung in die Charakterkunde*, Leipzig, 1929), who maintained that a man who is in part neurotic and ego-centric, and in part socio-centric, can be regarded as healthy in the latter part, and thus responsible for actions committed in *that* field; but not responsible for such as fall within the field of his diseased mind and are thus performed under neurotic compulsion. The position is, however, different with the moral evaluation of individual neurotic tendencies ('neurasthenic traits'), which, although weakening the will, do not take it away. They can by no means be looked upon as compulsory and free from guilt.

This brings us back to the question already touched upon in connection with Freud: To what extent can the psychology of the unconscious explain religion? From the Freudian standpoint, religion is nothing more than a neurotic sublimation of the *libido*. But, as we have already pointed out, the analyst, as analyst, has no right to represent any particular view of life. If the patient raises questions involving such views in the course of treatment the situation is naturally altered; a tempting possibility is then presented for achieving some positive influence. In spite of this however, experience has shown that the therapeutist must let the patient solve his own problems, or in the case of religious matters, must recommend him to consult his spiritual director. It would signify a deplorable lack of the proper scientific attitude if the therapeutist made use of his position to exert influence of a religious nature; for in this way he would be *depriving the patient of his responsibility to God* and thrusting him back into his neurosis. The methods of Jung are open to criticism from this angle; for he holds that the analyst should concern himself with the consequences of the patient's outlook upon life, and even advise him as to what sort of religion is most likely to help him. The result of such a treatment is that the patient imagines he has become religious, whereas in reality he has acquired psychological nourishment of no nutritious value. To explain the therapeutic value of religion is not to explain religion itself. If the therapeutist does not accept religion as a supernatural fact, it is his duty at least to respect this belief, which he does not do if he sees nothing but psychological value in religion. We admit freely that it may sometimes be necessary for the psychotherapeutist to analyse the religious position of the patient, if only to bring to light a subjective distortion of religion on his part. We have shown in an earlier work (van Lun and Ringel: *Seelsorge und Neurose*, 1951), that this kind of abuse of religion does really take place; and since then we have gathered further important material which tends to support this view. At the same time, we must never forget that serious difficulties for the psychotherapeutist are apt to arise in this field; for the patient will feel that, when it comes to religion, his opinions are as good as those of the doctor. This indicates the need for close co-operation between priest and psychotherapeutist.

It is hardly necessary to say that the priest should know what sort of an analytical treatment the doctor is employing, and that he should himself possess some knowledge of psychotherapy, so that he can explain to the patient in what way his religious life is influenced by his neurosis. The patient will then be in a position to realise that the priest, in matters of religion, is telling him the same thing that the psychotherapeutic specialist told him. This will strengthen his confidence in the analytical treatment. The duties of the psychotherapeutist in the religious field do not go beyond thus pointing out the manner in which neurotic tendencies distort religious life. When the treatment has reached a stage where the patient is able to understand and control different values, the therapeutist must entrust his re-education in the field of religion to the priest. If no priest is at hand, in the case of a Catholic patient, the doctor, if he is himself a Catholic, should then undertake this task, while explaining to the patient that the new relationship is not that of doctor and patient, but of one Catholic to another. But he cannot, of course, possess the authority proper to a priest in such a case. This situation is to be avoided whenever possible, as we have already made clear.

Therapeutists who take it upon themselves to analyse the

patient's religious life must be reminded that grace has ways of making itself felt which are beyond their power to measure. We must again emphasise in the most decided manner that analytical psychology is not competent to analyse in any way whatever the concept of God, although this has been attempted in various quarters (e.g.28a). All such attempts, whether they tend to support the Catholic viewpoint or to oppose it, must be rejected on the ground of a complete unsuitability of method.

This brings us very near to the question: Can the psychology of the unconscious become the modern means for the 'care of souls,' or even a substitute for religion? Anyone who possesses even a modest knowledge of religious matters knows that this is wholly out of the question. There are psychotherapeutists who look upon their psychology as a religion. But we need not say that from the Christian standpoint such an error must be completely rejected. It is our view that analytical psychology can do no more than establish a healthy state of mind, serving as a foundation for the free and conscious co-operation of the subject in his relation to the life of grace. In referring, as above, to relationship with God, we spoke solely from the viewpoint of our religious beliefs. We cannot deduce belief in God from the material of analytical psychology; it is not the business of the psychology of the unconscious to provide us with proofs of the existence of God. If this kind of argument is put forward as scientific, it is time to protest strongly. There will always be indications to be found when we study the human soul. There is no occasion to drag in analytical psychology, which operates upon quite another level, as compared with revealed truth. It would be an error to assert, for example, that one type of modern psychology is nearer to religion than another. We must hold to a completely objective scale of values in passing judgment upon the relative merits of psychological systems; it would be most unwise to judge such systems according to whether or not their corresponding attitudes towards life approximate to our own.

he fact of a positive tendency, which may appeal to us, does
ot signify that the scientific psychological background is reliable.
he most that could be said is that one kind of analytical psychology
 better fitted than another to create psychological conditions
vourable to the growth of grace and religion. And is not this but
nother way of saying that this method is more successful in
storing health to a neurotic patient? All systems which are
ffective in this sense have equal value: that is what they are for.
)ur decision for or against a particular psychological doctrine
-is it true or is it not true?—depends upon its scientific content.
his content has a value which is purely scientific and we cannot
y it is either near to religion or remote from it. Religious discip-
ne of any kind is out of place in this field, and we have no right
) expect corroboration—and still less a proof—of religious truths
om analytical psychology. There is only one truth and it cannot
e labelled; it is neither Thomistic, nor individual-psychological,
or psychoanalytical. Each must seek to find truth in his own
eld of work, beginning with the actual facts learned from his
anch of science. We should not be prepared to agree with
ünkel, who said: 'The psychology of character has, again and
gain, been illuminated and deepened by the wisdom of
hristianity.' We certainly believe that psychology and the study of
haracter cannot fail to lead us to results which will conform to the
uths of our religion, but not that the science of psychology
educes its doctrines from another field, that of revealed truth.
o do that is to bring it outside its field which is that of a natural
ience.

CHAPTER III.

THE CO-OPERATION OF PRIEST AND DOCTOR

IT IS AN UNDOUBTED FACT that in earlier times not only wer the guidance of souls and the care of spiritual health the concer of the priesthood, but also the care of bodily health. This applie not only to pre-Christian times but continued into the Middl Ages. The most important reason for this lay, possibly, in th problem of body and soul which is far from being a moder problem: it occupied the men of past centuries, in all probabilit to a much greater extent than it does the men of today. W know, too, that in earlier ages practically the whole field o knowledge lay in the hands of the clergy, so that it was a matte of course that the care of the body should be their concern. Wit the coming of specialisation, it was natural that the latter shoul find its own specialists. This was recognised by the Church which at a later date, forbade priests to practise medicine, except by special authorization.

Despite this separation, there remained a borderland betwee the care of souls and that of the body: the field of *psychic disorders* so recently explored by modern psychology. These disorder raise many problems infringing upon ground more usually claime by priests as their own. Are the clergy to give up this ground also This question can hardly be answered directly, either in a positive or negative sense. Some doctors would like to see priests thrus back wholly into the field of the purely spiritual, thus deprivin them entirely of the natural basis of their spiritual tasks. It i possible that the Protestant clergy would find themselves able t accept this position; but the Catholic priest is bound to protes against it on every occasion. The Catholic Church holds tha we should not only proclaim the Gospel and administer th

42

acraments, but that the work of the Church must be carried
n with the aid of every advantage that can possibly be derived
rom modern knowledge and the most up-to-date methods.
Catholics are thus bound to desire that priests should be equipped
with a knowledge of modern methods in pedagogy and psychology.
This standpoint has been expressed in a practical saying, not
perhaps altogether correct but current among priests: 'One must
believe like a Thomist and act like a Molinist.' We fully realise
hat the grace of God can do anything and everything, but we also
realise that this same grace makes use of our human powers.
With Catholics it is therefore a matter of principle that the priest
should not decry, in the care of souls, any aid which the modern
science of the unconscious can offer him.

Therefore, the priest must not cease to concern himself with the
souls of those suffering from psychic disorders, even though these
also need psychotherapeutic treatment. Nevertheless, as we sought
o show in another place (van Lun and Ringel: *Seelsorge und
Neurose*, 1951), it is an impossible task for a priest, even if he is
fully trained in analytical psychology, to carry out an analysis
himself. For this there are two main reasons: first, because we
frequently notice, in the case of neurotic patients, that, if they are
created by a psychotherapeutist who is not a doctor, they tend to
withdraw to the region of physical complaints where they can
escape from the authority of the analyst. The same situation would
arise if a priest were in charge. It is necessary in these cases, that
the psychotherapeutist should be a doctor also, or at least that
he should work in the closest association with a doctor. The
treatment of a neurosis belongs more especially to medical
psychology, not to general psychology. Should a priest desire
to deal with such a case himself the least that we can ask of him
is that he should be a trained doctor. The second reason is also
important: the phenomenon of so-called 'transference,' to which
we have referred in passing, is liable to be especially difficult for
he celibate clergy. (Cf. the later chapter of this study, dealing

with hysteria). The patient, during his treatment, transfer emotional reactions to the psychotherapeutist: the conflicts o his earlier life emerge from the subconscious, with the differenc that the emotional charges are re-directed towards the psychologis It is scarcely necessary to point out how dangerous this ma become, when the latter is a priest. Dr. Dessauer, (writing in th review *Geist und Leben* of December, 1951), described the positio very clearly: 'The relationship between the patient and a pries practising as his analyst often becomes so complex and so difficul to interpret that a proper dissolution of the transference, as demande by this type of analysis, can become impossible. It is a matter o experience that, even in the case of an ordinary individual and priest, a process of transference leads to the breaking off of th normal spiritual relationship between priest and individual There can be no doubt whatever that serious injury can resul to the individual or the patient (as the case may be) and, in th case of a neurosis, an increase of the disorder.' And again: 'Th conflict that can arise in this way can hardly be resolved withou a fresh psychotherapeutic treatment of a most thorough kind to liberate the patient from his morbid yearning for the uniqu relationship which he has experienced.'

It would be very difficult for a priest to practise psychotherap upon a patient and, at the same time, to act as a priest in regar to him. The boundary between the two fields of activity fluctuate a great deal and to draw a clear cut line is practically impossible This is especially so if the two activities are in the hands of on and the same person. However, we need not concern ourselve further with this problem, since we have rejected, on principle the idea of treatment by a priest. We can sum up by stating that it is of the utmost importance from both standpoints—tha of the patient and that of the priest—that the latter should *no* act as analyst.

From the foregoing it will be clear to the reader that there is only one satisfactory synthesis: a close co-operation between priest and psychotherapeutist. To effect this, the priest must possess insight into the course of the treatment and into the aims and purposes of the patient. If he wishes to co-operate with the doctor in curing the patient, he will point out clearly to the latter, at an early stage—that is, after a certain degree of progress by the doctor—just what it is that the patient seeks to achieve through his subjective religious attitude. The patient may then say: 'But, Father, you are saying the same thing about religion that the doctor said when he spoke of my health!' When the patient reaches the point of asking questions like: 'But how could it come about that ——?' the priest can feel that his work from now on will lie within his own field of spiritual welfare. We hope to demonstrate this later. The question may be raised: Does not the priest interfere, after all, with the analysis, by making use of a kind of analysis of his own, so that the patient experiences a double form of treatment? The answer is that such an attitude on the part of the priest does not constitute treatment. The priest must know how his penitent conducts his life; he must examine his guiding principles. This needs no analysis. The doctor can inform him; or, if he has sufficient experience in the psychology of the subconscious, he can discover what he needs through conversation with the patient. The doctor may be able to tell him, or the patient may himself tell him, how these guiding principles came to be formed. Then he will be in a position to judge how the patient arrived at his false religious notions; for example, how he transferred his father—or mother—images into the religious field. Then—and then only—he can make it clear to the patient that his neurotic condition is really making itself felt in his religious life; that he is abusing religion for his own purposes. It is true that the doctor could also point this out to him; but he has little authority outside his own field, and the patient is therefore inclined to look upon religious life as a sphere of refuge when pressed by the doctor—just as he will retreat into the physical field if he is analysed by a priest. Should the doctor seek to influence

the patient in anything which concerns religion, the latter is sur
to say that the doctor does not understand him and that, whateve
he may say, the matter under discussion was a genuine religiou
experience. The priest alone can undertake this task successfully
But it does not constitute the practice of psychotherapy; it come
rather under the head of an approach to the priest's proper spiritua
task. It will, however, have therapeutic value; for it will hinde
the patient's escapist efforts.

On the other hand, the doctor's work in psychotherapy mus
not be regarded as a form of spiritual direction. It is the cure o
disease, not the care of souls. The doctor's work is to lead th
patient back to a healthy state of mind and body; to remove th
elements causing mental distortion. This paves the way for th
patient to achieve a healthy attitude towards religious matter
But such a result cannot be regarded as a *necessary* consequence
since the acceptance of religious truths, even when a healthy so
has been prepared, is and always must be dependent upon th
grace of God. It cannot be asserted, without strong dissent, tha
psychotherapy is the 'handmaid of theology,' as was once sai
of philosophy. The religion of the patient is no concern of th
psychotherapeutist. If he feels a personal interest in the religiou
attitude of his patient, this can be made known only in his capacit
as a Christian, not as a doctor. If he finds it necessary to appea
to the moral order, because breaches of this order have given ris
to neurotic states through bringing the patient into conflict wit
the community, he need not do so from religious motives. A
most, he draws attention to the marvellous works and laws o
nature; and on this foundation grace may operate.

*   *   *   *   *

It will be useful to illustrate the practical co-operation of prie
and doctor by means of a few examples. Under no circumstance
—this should be made clear at the start—will the priest revea
anything confided to him in the confessional. It is strongl

dvised that he should *not* do this, even if the consent of the patient
as been obtained; although, of course, the priest may consult
he doctor, with the consent of the patient, about any matters
which the latter may have told him outside the confessional.
The relationship between doctor and priest must be based upon the
priest's knowledge of the type of treatment being practised by the
doctor; similarly, the doctor will know what kind of aid is being
given to his penitent by the priest. What is needed is mutual
confidence, much independent work on both sides, and good
co-ordination. In the following case-histories, the seal of the
confessional is in no case broken, and medical secrecy is protected
by such alterations as will make identification impossible.

A young man, now thirty years old, the son of a farmer and
at present a student of philosophy, was very strictly brought up
from early infancy. He was constantly threatened with punishment
and, in fact, was often beaten for the smallest offences. At the age
of five, he remembers being severely flogged by his father because
he had been seen playing with his sexual organs. As he grew up,
he was never allowed any independence; he had to ask permission
for the smallest things and never had the feeling that he was free.
His family was strictly Catholic and the father habitually connected
his rigid educational ideas with his religion, so that the boy grew
up to equate the idea of *father* with the concept of *religion*. As the
years went on, the sense of grievance felt towards the over strict
father became stronger, and this attitude was naturally enough
extended to the Church which he had been brought up to identify
with the father. Here we have an excellent example of how a
mistake in the educational field on the natural level can be the
cause of grave damage to the religious life—a fact which must
never be overlooked by educators. We shall consider this matter
in some detail in the following section. In the case of this patient
the wrong father-son relationship was the clear cause of a deep
disturbance of religious life.

The young student was drawn into the war and experienced a

sensation of being liberated from the yoke imposed upon him ;
home. The result was that he lost no time in systematicall
abusing his newly won liberty. He practised self-abuse mor
frequently, as well as having relations with women from tim
to time. When he came home on occasional visits he again too
over the rôle of complete subservience, and played the rôle of goo
Catholic, as his father desired. When the war was over, he began t
study and became friendly with a Catholic girl whose mothe
was a Protestant and whose Catholicism was not of the strictes
He became engaged to her. This choice was no accident—a poin
the priest may note—for it corresponded exactly to his inwar
position and conflict. Like himself, the girl was outwardly Catholic
but ready to go against the teachings of the Church. The studen
persuaded her that more things were permissible than the priest
admitted. Although actual intercourse did not take place, h
induced the girl to take part in acts of exposure of a more o
less indecent nature. Finally, however, he confessed all this t
a priest; but when the latter told him his conduct was sinfu
the latent hostility of the student against the Church broke ou
afresh. He now hated the priest and the Church. Some tim
later, he underwent treatment, because his manifest neurosis gav
rise to serious anti-social manifestations. He avoided his home
because his parents opposed his engagement, and he quarrelle
with his relations and friends, who, in their turn, described hin
as 'quite impossible.' Every now and then, he sought out a pries
and explained to him that, when he had been with the girl, hi
bad habit of self-abuse slackened off, and for this reason he di
not regard his relations with the girl as sinful. He seems to hav
expected the priest to accept this view and to admit that wha
he did was not sinful, and he complained bitterly about the 'rigi
attitude' of the Church, which reminded him of his father.

The task of the psychotherapeutist, in this case, was to discove
by analysis the source of these conflicts, and to reveal the origin
of the childish aberrations, thereby making clear to the patien

hat he was pursuing false aims, and bringing his real motives
before his mind. Furthermore, he must direct him away from
his anti-social attitude and bring him back to a life integrated
with that of the community, so that he is fit to master the central
tasks of his life. The priest's task, on the other hand, is to point
out to him how his attitude towards the priesthood and the Church
has been developed: the patient has transferred to God the special
complex which dominated him in respect of his father. He wants
to break away from the commandments—unless they agree with
his wishes—because his attitude up to the present has been: 'As
long as I can make use of the commandments and of God, I will
do what they say, but if they stand in my path, away with them!'
The patient fails to realise that God and the commandments
possess an *objective* value. The priest should help him to understand that the priest to whom he made his confession had assumed
for him the likeness of his father from the very moment that he
ought to forbid his actions as sinful, because his father's constant
prohibitions had been the main factor in his upbringing. The
reason for his hatred of this priest thus becomes clear. Further,
he should be able to understand that he had never recognised,
in the right fashion, the commandments of God and God Himself
in His infinite majesty. His religion was no more than lip-service.
Later on, the patient will place before the psychotherapeutist
the question of his guilt; but this is the affair of the priest and not
of the doctor. The priest should indicate to him that his sin consists,
above all, in his *attitude* towards God, and that his sinful acts are
merely an expression of this wrong attitude. Looked at from this
angle, it is not so much the acts (the self-abuse, the indecent
exposures, etc.), that constituted his sin, but far more his misuse
of God and His laws, of which the sins were *symptoms*. It has been
pointed out by many great masters of the spiritual life in the past,
that it is good for our spiritual life to confess our *basic* spiritual
error—the error from which the others stem. The process we have
here described is nothing other than a modification of this ancient

method. It is at about this point that the patient can be expected
to bring to light the whole tangle of his religious difficulties; fo
the treatment releases a dynamism which causes him to experienc
these problems with a new and intensive force. He will begin to
feel that the faith which he has hitherto had is wholly useless and
devoid of value; although, on the other hand, he may want to
return to it.

At this point, the priest will find that he is confronted with
serious task which he must perform alone, without the aid of th
doctor. In the first place, he must point out to the penitent tha
the faith which he now considers useless will always retain it
objective value, and even now—although he has turned against i
—still possesses validity and imposes its responsibilities upon him
A negative experience of faith is not of necessity always negative
The commandments which, hitherto, he accepted only whe
they suited him, have nevertheless a positive constructive an
objective force which demands his obedience. The priest mus
remind him of the objective value of the sacraments for him a
for others. The patient will then naturally enquire if he is no
liable *again* to abuse religion and the moral law. This possibilit
certainly exists and is even a probability. It must, therefore, b
pointed out that, to achieve any permanent result, a gradu:
and sustained effort is needed. At the same time it is a fact, whic
we have seen corroborated many times, that a patient, after hi
eyes have been opened to the erroneous nature of the previou
conduct of his life and to the possibility of making a fresh sta
on positive lines, quite suddenly gives up the bad habits of h
former life—such as self-abuse, lying, stealing, etc.—because no
he realises that such things are no longer of any *use* to him. Ther
may, of course, be a certain amount of backsliding now an
then. But with religion itself, with the commandments an
the sacraments, and with belief in God, the matter is less simpl
The priest will need a great deal of patience and understanding
but he will be recompensed by the great joy attached to this nobl

work. It must be emphasised that the priest must make it clear to his penitent, again and again, that, if he wants to experience his religion in its newly won fulness and richness, he must go down on his knees and pray earnestly to God. This is contained in the concept of faith itself: for this faith is a free gift of God.

The patient must gradually be brought back to a right relationship with God, a relationship which, as we saw in the preceding chapter, will certainly be of great value in causing the neurosis to disappear completely. It will be very good for the patient if later he expresses a desire to make a general Confession of interior sins. This can take place only if the priest has always shewn an understanding for his position, while not permitting the penitent under his guidance to misuse his religion. Under these circumstances, the priest will be the first point of contact for the patient in finding his way back to health and a right life within the community. This result will be due to the doctor, the priest, and the grace of God.

Naturally, complete success cannot always be obtained. We will give one or two examples. A priest of some sixty years was sent to the doctor; he had great difficulty with his breviary, needing some hours to read it. Often he made use of a German translation and read it at the same time; he did not then experience the same inhibitions. But he knew that in this way he was not performing his whole duty. Formerly, he had had the same difficulty with the Mass and some other duties. His condition became clear when he said that he found himself unable to do anything laid upon him as a *duty*, but if it was an act of free will he could manage it quite well. Good reports of his work during his long term of priesthood had always been received, and he still attended in a satisfactory manner to his various tasks. He had a small parish where he was a person of importance. Every therapeutic specialist will agree with us when we say that, in such a case, an analysis offers almost no chance of success. The patient is too old and could not draw upon sufficient vitality to alter

himself. As in the case of other illnesses, a neurosis of long standing
is more difficult to cure, and hence it is most important for
neurotic to seek treatment without delay. In this respect th
priest can frequently help by recognising in good time, the tru
state of the patient, and persuading him of the necessity for treat
ment. In the above case, the best that can be done by the docto
and the priest is to procure for the sufferer a dispensation, in view
of the special circumstances; or, if the priest who works with th
doctor has sufficient authority with his brother priest, he ca
persuade him that he need not go through with the normal breviar
duties in view of his state of health. For the patient himself i
might be best for his Bishop to give this dispensation.

The following is another case where a priest had to interven
with a limited objective in view. A woman of fifty, who looke
nearer seventy, was sent by her doctor to the priest. At the ag
of thirty-five—that is before the proper time—she suffered he
climacteric with cessation of menstruation. She was very pious
attended every possible service and received Communion, whe
possible, every day. One day, while at a Communion service
she experienced a strong sexual orgasm, and this was subsequently
repeated many times. We need hardly explain that the poo
woman saw herself as defrauded by life itself of her possibilities i
the field of sex and reacted to this with a strong neurotic symptom
Nor need we dwell upon the reasons which impelled her to seek
out a psychotherapist or the further development of the neurosis
It is sufficient to explain that it was impossible to help this woma
at her age in any really fundamental way. One might be abl
to convince her that her plan of life was false, but, in that case, a
number of the rules governing her life and established for many
years, would be done away with, and one can say, with som
confidence, that the patient would not be able to set up new rule
of life. The best advice that the priest can give her is that she shoul
not exaggerate her religious devotions and that she should *no*
go to Communion too often in future. He should then mak

clear to her that what happened to her is in no sense sinful, since it did not occur through her volition. He should and *must* leave the rest to the grace of God. Of such cases, with a limited objective, Rümke says that they may not represent the most important or striking tasks of the psychotherapist; but in a practical sense, they are of great value.

Even in cases which are in themselves hopeful the treatment does not *always* succeed. For one reason or another the analysis does not go according to plan. And even when it is successful, the analysis alone is not a cure. The patient may attain to an insight into his own psychology, but this may bring to light a strain of marked fatalism. The explanation of the case, according to the pattern of an analysis, is not in itself enough; the patient may know what is the matter and yet fail to overcome his problem. The act of understanding must be followed up by a positive assimilation and effort. The Austrian psychologist Caruso has this in mind, in his work on psycho-analysis (Herder, Vienna, 1952), where he speaks of a necessary 'existential synthesis.'

The work of therapy makes great demands upon both doctor and patient, and it cannot be brought to a satisfactory conclusion without the active co-operation of the patient. It is a disastrous error to believe that the doctor alone can effect a cure: no one can dispense the patient from the contribution that he himself must make. But there are patients who cannot do this. It is very dangerous to promise more than can be performed. Psychotherapy is not a panacea; not a few neuroses remain uninfluenced. Prognosis depends upon the type of neurosis, the time during which the illness has existed, the personality of the patient as a whole, and, needless to say, upon his attitude towards the treatment and upon its progress. We are compelled to admit that in many cases therapy fails to answer our expectations. In other cases, there is a certain improvement often due to suggestion but no real cure. But in such cases, we must not underrate the success achieved, for even a measure of relief means a great deal to the sufferer.

What we ask is that, in all cases, some treatment at least should be given. An *a priori* assumption of failure in the treatment of neurosis must never be admitted. Our belief in life itself is too strong to tolerate such defeatism.

A few words are necessary as to the *wrong* relationship between doctor and priest. The kind of mistake the priest is liable to make will already be fairly clear from the foregoing. But a distinction must be made between priests who have had some training in modern psychology and those who have not. The latter will be called upon for their co-operation only in cases where they have sent one of their flock to the doctor, realising that he needed that sort of medical attention. In the case of the priest who has had training, a considerable danger exists that, side by side with the doctor's analysis, he will attempt an analysis of his own. This leads, with the utmost inevitability, to the failure of both analyses. The untrained priest must follow carefully the directions of the doctor, while avoiding on the one hand an over-emphasis of the patient's responsibility, and on the other hand a rejection of this sense of responsibility. His most important duty will be to encourage the penitent and to point out that it is his duty to seek treatment, since this offers him the only possibility of getting at the roots of his sin and curing it thoroughly.

The doctor, too, is of course liable to make mistakes in this work of co-operation. We are reminded of the following case. A young priest without any special knowledge of modern psychological methods, but having heard of the importance of a right treatment in certain cases, sent one of his penitents to a psychotherapist. The young patient, who could not overcome his habit of self-abuse, went to the doctor and the latter wrote to the priest saying that he had done well to send him the patient. He did not consider (he added) that the patient committed any serious sin through his habit, and expressed the view that the priest could, without hesitation, grant him absolution whenever the matter was raised. The doctor then told the young man that he should come and see him again in a few months and tell him how he was getting on. This was the whole extent of the treatment. It must be added that the therapeutist was a convinced Catholic. Quite apart from the fact that the priest could hardly reply to this letter, being bound by the seal of the confessional, we may note that the priest would take good care never again to send a penitent to a doctor who was not prepared even to attempt the treatment of a young patient, in a case of a decidedly hopeful nature. Moreover, the doctor took it upon himself to pass a moral judgment, thus going outside his competence. One is compelled to believe that he, like many others, took the view that self-abuse is normal with young people. The term 'normal' might be employed in the sense of frequently occurring, and with this judgment we should have to agree; but we could not accept the term, if employed in the sense that no judgment of a moral kind can attach to the practice. In this view we are supported by Pope Pius XII who, in a speech to Catholic doctors, sharply condemned this outlook on the problem. Doctors must not forget that priests and the Church as a whole will never surrender the right to form moral judgments. The doctor has the right to persuade a priest that, in many cases, there is really no cause for moral blame; but he cannot relieve the priest of the moral duties and responsibilities attaching to his office as the spiritual director of the patient. A further possible error on the part of the doctor, endangering a right co-operation with the priest must be pointed out here: unfortunately it is committed by many Catholic doctors. A neurosis case is sent by a priest to a Catholic nerve specialist. The latter listens to what the patient tells him about his troubles, which threaten to destroy his entire social existence, and then asks: 'Are you a faithful Catholic?' The patient says: 'Yes.' The doctor replies: 'Then you should accept your neurosis as a cross sent you by God and bear it patiently: the sooner you begin, the more quickly you will find it bearable.' Apart from the fact that such an attitude cannot be justified from the medical standpoint, it would appear to be positively dangerous. We have frequently found that patients who had received such advice developed, as a reaction, a violent opposition to religion, since they felt that it aimed at the 'perpetuation' of their disorder. It is easy to see that a priest cannot be helped by his association with such a doctor, since he carries out no treatment and does no more than tell the patient (thus going outside his proper sphere) something that the priest himself could have said, were it needful. In this connection, the priest should be warned against too readily saying that this or that disorder should be accepted and patiently endured, or words to that effect: it is essential, first of all, to examine the matter and discover if it is really a case of necessary unavoidable suffering, of a trial imposed by God, or whether the man is being tormented by symptoms of a disorder from which he could be liberated by the right therapeutic treatment. We have already spoken of the danger of one-sided supernaturalism on the part of the priest; now is the time to issue a warning against supernaturalism on the part of Catholic doctors. Unfortunately one continually meets with priests who, as a result of their own mistaken attitude, listen too readily to such doctors, thus becoming even more mistaken.

In the co-operation of priest and doctor, the latter commits a grave blunder if he imagines that the insight into his wrong attitude or sin which a patient can obtain through an analysis is the same thing as repentance, and therefore regards the patient as now exculpated. To realise that one has made mistakes or committed sins is very far from being the same thing as to experience true repentance, knowing that one has sinned against the infinite majesty of God. The difference between the therapeutic and the sacramental effect has been excellently described by J. Miller (cf. his book: *Katholische Beichte und Psychotherapie*; Tyrolia Verlag, Innsbruck, Vienna, 1947). The priest is the only man who, by virtue of his divine calling, can accept repentance, forgive sins, and explain that they have been forgiven. No therapeutic practitioner, no matter what his own religious position may be, can do this. And he must never forget that a priest cannot allow himself to be thrust back into the position of a mere exorcist. There is only one danger that can result in this fashion: the priest —as we have already indicated—may start studying psycho-therapeutic literature and try out his theories on the patient. This can have serious results, endangering the patient's hopes of recovery. But a far worse consequence can follow, if the doctor endangers the religious faith of the patient, by seeking to substitute some kind of psychological belief or system. The only genuine solution is a truly harmonious co-operation of doctor and priest. This kind of co-operation will become more and more important in the near future. It will make an essential contribution to the mental and moral health of the whole community, from its smallest element, the family, up to the biggest, the state. To take a single example, the organisation *Caritas* in Vienna has made use of these methods in its special branch, offering help and advice to all those who are tired of life. Their success has been unquestionable. This branch of good works seeks to restore to a sound psychic state those who have lost their grip on life, and to restore a religious outlook to the many who desire to get back what they have lost. In this connection, we refer the reader to the studies on suicide by E. Ringel. Many non-Catholic medical specialists have borne witness on numerous occasions, to the importance of religion for those in danger of suicide, and to the new influx of strength they can thus receive. This knowledge, which applies to many other branches of psychic hygiene, forms the very foundation of the efficacy and utility of co-operation between priest and doctor.

The ideal pattern of this co-operation could be enlarged through drawing upon the aid of suitable social welfare organisations. The social aspect is in itself very necessary in the task of saving souls. In a multitude of cases, social conditions have a great deal of influence. Let us not forget the words of Thomas Aquinas, that *a certain measure of material well-being is necessary in order to live a religious life.* If the necessary possibilities for this life are lacking, it is not possible, apart from a special grace, to be and remain religious. The human mind is apt to be driven into opposition by need. Throughout the whole of life, from childhood onwards, social troubles, poverty and want play a vital part in intensifying neurotic conflicts.

We have seen that the overcoming of psychic disorders is an important factor in the care of souls; yet we cannot say that the task of the psychology of the unconscious in the field of spiritual welfare ends with this. The priest will be able to make use of his enlarged knowledge acquired through modern psychology not *only* in relation to disordered minds, but in relation to *every human being with whom he comes into contact.* Every single individual would like to be approached from the angle of his own particular psychology. Through the study of analytical psychology we find ourselves able to fulfil this desire. We note that a young person, more especially, will participate with enthusiasm in the task of his own formation, seeking to find out what is the trend of his own unconscious urge. This has two consequences: 1. The authority of the priest over youth is strengthened; he can exert a powerful religious influence, since young people will be more likely to accept his spiritual leadership, and in this way young men and women can be won over to the Church for their whole lives 2. He will be able to relieve the community and fellow-priests of the burden of a possible future neurotic case.

CHAPTER IV.

THE PSYCHOLOGY OF FAITH

'YOU WORK IN A FIELD THAT IS VERY DIFFICULT. BUT
YOUR ACTIVITY IS CAPABLE OF ACHIEVING VALUABLE RESULTS
FOR MEDICINE, FOR THE KNOWLEDGE OF THE SOUL IN
GENERAL, FOR THE RELIGIOUS DISPOSITIONS OF MAN AND
FOR THEIR DEVELOPMENT.' (Pius XII in his address to the
Congress of Psychotherapists).

THE SPIRITUAL DIRECTOR must see the man of the modern age
as he really is, and not as he would like to see him. In the opinion
of the well-known Catholic writer, Bishop Sheen, our apologetical
literature is fifty years behind the times, because this point has
been overlooked. Arguments employed by priests in their
apologetical work, which were effective not many years ago,
have suddenly ceased to be effective. The interior life of the man
of today is so confused that he simply cannot grasp them.

The scientific world is bound to do its utmost to aid priests in
their efforts to explain why the capacity for faith has so rapidly
diminished, and why the warnings and advice of our spiritual
leaders fall again and again upon deaf ears. The most important
of all the contributions science can make must come from the
field of analytical psychology. What must be done is very simple.
We must use the utmost diligence and patience in collecting
particulars of specific cases, one after the other, always asking the
same question: Can we, in studying the dynamic development of
psychic life, find particular situations which exercise a decisive
influence on the attitude to the Church.

We propose to devote more particular attention in the future
to this special method of studying the development of psychic
disorder. A few characteristic relationships have emerged from
what we already know. But before we consider two selected

case-histories, we should like to deal with an objection which we feel sure is already arising in the minds of some priests as they read this chapter. In making use of such a method, do we not degrade religion from the supernatural to the merely natural level? In reply, we must repeat that, in making such studies, we do not for a moment deny or overlook the operations of grace; but it is clear that in scientific investigation of this kind, we are forced to leave them on one side, because, by their very nature, they are not subject to measurement or control. Moreover we can find support in the oft-quoted saying: *Gratia supponit naturam*, which has been the subject of such a multitude of comments that we need not add to them.

Finally, our attempt to discover, by scientific means, the natural reasons for the rapid decline in religious faith, seems to us to be no more than the logical consequence of a development that began when Thomas Aquinas introduced Aristotelian methods into theology. Despite the extreme rationalism which lurks behind the method of Aristotle, the saintly scholar ventured to bring it into the closest union with the Christian revelation. Aquinas drew a sharp line dividing nature and super-nature, and yet he saw both as united through the *potentia oboendientalis*, the power of obedience, or more accurately, the indwelling urge to obey, on the part of nature in relation to super-nature. The result of this is a complete system of order and harmony embracing the whole of life. Lower life, acting in accordance with its own nature, yields itself to the higher, and serves its ends, while the higher takes possession of the lower and allows it become an instrument of its purpose. L. Soukup in his work, *Geopferte Natur* (Herder, Freiburg and Vienna, 1941), comments usefully on this theme: 'For the continuance of a higher life on the natural level would not be possible, unless the sphere of vegetative life with its entire *activity* were prepared, in its own way, to co-operate, for without a minimum of such co-operation the higher life could not exist or maintain itself. The same pattern applies to the human sphere, where the life of the senses must support the spiritual life, not only in a passive sense but with the whole of its intensity and activity, so that the spiritual can reach the summit of its development. In the same way the mental and spiritual must subordinate itself to the supernatural, to the life of grace. The highest form of activity which the mental and spiritual can develop is to be found in *conscious free decision*. Here alone is the full manifestation of spiritual activity to be seen. In other words man's highest and most genuine activity is revealed in a personal act; that is to say, in a *creative* act, springing from the inmost core and effective centre of a spiritual being—a person. The life of super-nature, of grace, can flower only when it is supported by personal acts, by means of which man continually permits the freely working grace of God to move him to free decisions.'

This leaves us with a concrete and precise pattern of questions for our investigations. We have to discover how this capacity for being moved by grace in personal acts, this fitting of the self into the pattern of divine order, came to be lost. It is clear that such a method of investigation transfers the centre of gravity of our work to the field of the rational and psychological. The danger that, in this way, the predominant factor, the supernatural and revealed, should be overlooked, seems to us to be removed by the simple fact that the investigators are themselves faithful Catholics.

★   ★   ★   ★   ★

Let us examine a case-history. The patient was a young woman of twenty-seven years, the daughter of highly respected people of the so-called 'better classes.' Her parents lived, to all appearances, harmoniously together. The father, a man of fundamentally gentle character, although subject to swift changes of mood and occasional outbursts of temper, was intellectually inferior to the mother. The latter played a dominating part in all business affairs. She was a woman who tolerated no opinion but her own; she

was pedantic, strict, very conscientious and always 'correct.'
We realise, already, that the harmony in this marriage was no
more than an appearance. Behind a façade of normal and happy
life, a condition of powerful tension existed between man and
wife. The patient, an only child, felt herself drawn to the father,
for reasons which may not be demonstrable logically, but which
can be deduced, with a high degree of probability, from a consideration of certain factors. The girl was obviously repelled by the
excessive strictness of her mother, who was otherwise fitted to
play the male rôle in a child's mind better than the father. We
know from a study of Freud's psychology that children, in general,
are inclined to be attracted towards the parent of the opposite sex
—an observation which we may regard as having adequate scientific
support. At any rate the father became the girl's ideal, the object
of her devotion and a subject for imitation. The girl became
in every respect very similar to her father (analysts call this process
'identification'), a result which seems to shake the hitherto accepted
domination of the theory of heredity. As a child, the girl was,
like her father, ultra-sensitive, easily irritated and unstable in her
moods. At the age of seven, a catastrophe overtook the family.
For the first time the father—possibly with the notion of asserting
his independence and breaking away from the domination of the
mother—undertook important business transactions, without even
telling his wife what was going on. He blundered seriously and
the family fortunes were wrecked. He felt unable to tell his wife,
suffered severely from pangs of conscience, felt unequal to the
situation, and seeing no way out, took his own life. From that
moment, the girl's inner life went astray and her development
became disordered. Before relating the further events a few words
of comment will be useful.

Analytical psychology has performed a highly important service
in throwing light upon the immense importance of family life.
This case clearly demonstrates that the breakdown of family life
was responsible for the catastrophe and the psychic disorder

following upon it. It is not so much a question of the outer framework of the family as of its inner meaning and value. When the harmony of father and mother is destroyed, the child suffers spiritual damage. Every analytical psychologist, no matter what school he may belong to or what his outlook on life may be, will reply in answer to the question: What must we do to prevent psychic disorders? 'Build up a strong and harmonious family life.'

When actual cases of psychic disorder are studied in the light of analytical psychology, we look for causal connections. This enables us to discover reasons why the psychic life of the patient went astray. In the above case, for example, amongst other reasons, there was the suicide of the father. This case offers a good example of the injustice of the charge, often brought against the psycho-analytical school, that it explains developments in personality as determined by causes outside control—that is, along materialistic lines. For, firstly, it is false to believe that psychic disorder can be explained by reference to a single factor. It has been emphasised by Hoff and others that a single specific shock (*trauma*) should never be held responsible for a neurosis, but rather a number of factors, all working together to produce a shock effect. In our present case, we could select as an additional factor the tension within the family, which undoubtedly caused unnoticed damage to the child in her early formative years, long before the suicide of the father. Secondly, it must be clear without further argument that a vital difference exists between the kind of psychic causation found here and the purely deterministic causality existing in the field of physical reality. If one drops a stone it *must* take the course prescribed by gravity. But nobody is likely to assert that when a father commits suicide, the daughter *must* suffer the effects noted later in this case. A shock of this kind is a danger which can all too easily give rise to disorder, but it need not necessarily do so. The manner in which the person concerned deals *inwardly* with the event is the decisive factor. Even Freud admits this, for he states, in one place, that many infantile scenes of significance in the analysis of neurosis are not reproduced as memories in the mind of the patient, but are the result of a re-construction. Thus, tendencies are at work which are apparently able to alter events after their occurrence, and to falsify experiences, so that they are no longer remembered and felt in the manner in which they really took place, but in a fashion adapted to the specific structure of the subject's personality. The upshot of all this is that the experience, inward construction, and actions of the patient combine to form a tendenciously coloured picture of the events. The original factors—in this case, the family situation and the suicide—are compressed into a pattern, and, later on, other new events will be fitted into this pre-arranged form. This pattern of reaction is in harmony with certain specific aspects of the subject's life and will unroll itself like a reflex action, almost automatically. As Weizsacker points out, these laws of nature have their own appropriate paths, but they have power over us only under certain circumstances. When one gets into a train, the speed, the times of arrival and departure, and the stopping places are determined for one; they have power over one; but what is *not* determined is whether one gets into the train at all.

Let us return to our patient. She has got into her train. We shall see at what stations she arrives. We will give a time-table:

12 years old—she steals from her mother.

16 years old—she indulges in fraud and goes about with men.

22 years old—she marries a criminal and then gets a divorce.

24 years old—she gets two good posts and loses both of them, while utterly neglecting her children.

25 years old—she takes to crime—theft and swindling—and is arrested.

26 years old—she becomes a secret prostitute.

Some details of the journey: after the death of her father, the girl's reserved attitude towards her mother—which had existed throughout her childhood—developed into a positive hatred. Without being conscious of her reasons, she held it against the mother that she had not been able to prevent the fatal step taken by the father; that she had failed in her duty. It is possible that she looked upon the father as being sacrificed by the mother, who was the dominant partner. At any rate, the child made things as difficult as she could for the mother and rapidly became a marked example of the unmanageable child. At the age of twelve, the first crass symptoms appeared; she began to steal all sorts of little things from her mother. That this was not done for the sake of the articles taken is proved by the fact that they were things of no value to the child herself, but they were for some reason important to the mother. These acts constituted a species of attack upon the mother, a means of giving expression to hatred. It is interesting to note that the time when these acts began was not accidental. They began at the exact moment when the mother, wanting to earn some money, had taken a post in a branch of social service. The girl's reply to this was to perform flagrantly anti-social acts. It was her aim to expose her mother, to make an outcast, to drag her down—as she more than succeeded in doing a little later. During the next four years, the patient travelled at a high speed along the same track. She was now planning to employ her powerful, awakening sexual life in the furtherance of her unchanging aims. She told fantastic stories about herself, made a host of friends and sometimes stayed out all night. The warnings, exhortations, and punishments of the mother were all useless. When twenty-two years old she married a work-shy fellow, whom she knew to be engaged in crime. The mother sought desperately to stop the affair, but was silenced by discovering that her daughter was pregnant. The next thing was a change of tactics. The girl acted as if she did not want to marry. This plunged the mother, who dreaded the birth of an illegitimate child, into such a state that she again and again implored the girl to marry this man. Finally, the marriage did take place, but it was already obvious that it could not endure and would end in divorce. The daughter now began to attack her mother, on the ground that it was she who drove her into this disastrous marriage. She had now succeeded in creating a situation such that she could, with a show of reason, charge her mother with being the cause of her downfall. All such charges were, of course, substitutes for the real charge, of which she was not conscious: that the mother was to blame for her father's death.

The following stage of her journey saw a remarkable development: although divorced she did not separate from her husband and under his influence drifted further into the world of crime. We can understand the cause of this. She had to maintain a situation enabling her to reproach her mother with her 'substitute-charge,' and she had to do this as long as she herself did not recognise the actual ground of reproach. Accordingly, she went on living with her former husband and even had other children by him, so that she could turn to her mother and say: 'You have destroyed my life, not only for a period, but for years on end—in fact forever; for it was you who drove me into this marriage.'

The patient took not the slightest interest in her children; she did not even enquire what became of them. But when one of them died in a home, she brought violent charges against the management on the ground of alleged neglect. We would not be wrong in assuming that these charges were directed, fundamentally, against *herself*; that she felt a sense of guilt and that she again made use of a substitute, of a person who could be reproached instead of herself.

Meanwhile, the patient had made very good progress in her professional work, and obtained an excellent post. But after a time her peculiar mentality made itself felt again; with no good reason she threw up her work, but by a stroke of luck got another position. She did not stay long; she absconded with money belonging to her employers, and for a while lived a gay life swindling hotels, etc. But, before long, she gave herself up to the police and confessed, not only to her own misdeeds, but to various crimes committed by her former husband. She served a sentence in prison and was released. We take occasion at this point to mention the great importance of a knowledge of analytical psychology to the *prison* chaplain. It is often very difficult to approach prison cases; yet they await someone who can understand them and help them to a better way of life. Only very rarely can they be influenced by direct religious means; they have usually wandered too far afield for that. One must approach them from the human and psychological side. Co-operation between the prison priest, on the one hand, and a team of workers helping released prisoners, on the other, could perform a difficult but, despite everything, a very hopeful work. In Vienna the *Caritas* organisation is creating such a team.

The sentence was according to law and we do not suggest that a just punishment should be avoided in such cases of psychic disorder. What we do assert, however, is that the mere fact of being put in prison for a certain period will not cure a neurosis or solve a conflict. On the contrary, the patient left the prison more embittered, more aggressive, and more stubborn than she had ever been previously. She refused to accept any aid from her mother or anyone else. She said she would look after herself, and lost no time in beginning her life as a secret prostitute.

This complicated and outwardly incomprehensible string of events can be brought together under a relatively simple head. The patient, when a child, suffered a series of shocks and finally, through the suicide of her father, she arrived at a state of mind causing her to be dominated by a single powerful conviction. This can be summed up in a sentence: *My father let me down.* All her subsequent actions were performed under the influence of a single slogan, crystallising her secret (that is her *subconscious*) plan of life: *Just as my father let me down, so I am going to let all of you down.* The first to suffer was the mother, blamed as we know for what happened to the father, and betrayed to the last possible limit; next came her husband; then followed the children. All were let down. Her profession did not escape; she let that down too. And ultimately she let herself down. She threw away the last shreds of human dignity she possessed: she sold herself.

*   *   *   *   *

We have dealt with this case in some detail for a special reason. It is not difficult to read between the lines the presence of another problem going beyond the purely psychological. This was the failure on the part of the patient to develop a normal religious life. First let us make clear that we are not dragging the religious issue into this strange case: it was the patient herself who brought the matter up. She explained that, as a small child, she liked going to church, but at a later date—she does not know how it happened—she became alienated from the outward life of religion and, finally, came to be convinced that religious life was a 'piece of theatricality,' and declared herself to have no belief of any kind. Her parents, especially the mother, and also her school teachers did not fail to impart religious instruction; but at a later date she reacted like a bull to a red rag towards anything connected with religion. She refused even to discuss religious matters, saying, 'Even to talk about religion makes me feel quite sick.'

Many of our readers will no doubt think that such a woman as this could never be induced to lead a life of faith. They may perhaps say it is a pity to waste valuable time and effort on 'such people.' Yet, on the other hand, we know with absolute certainty that every priest is a follower of the same Christ who went out to save the lost sheep, and who found more joy in one sinner who was saved than in ninety-nine just persons. Moreover, cases like this are now legion. We selected an extreme example in order to offer a vivid picture of a psychology leading to the rejection of faith. Similar case-histories without number, less dramatic in form, and exhibiting, very likely, only one or two isolated symptoms, can be found to point in the same direction.

To sum up: we have seen that our patient, as the result of feeling herself let down, resolved to do the same to everybody else. She went to the furthest extreme: she let God down. When her father died she had a grievance against the 'good God' of her childhood days. He was all-powerful, but *He did not save her father.* Later on she rejected God, turned away from Him, and even mocked Him. All this was done consciously, even if the real motives moving her were never precisely clear to her mind. This is illustrated by the fact that, when questioned as to her reasons for such a hatred of religion, she was not able to produce anything more than a few empty phrases.

At this point, a most pertinent question may be asked. A great many children have experienced the death of a person dear to them, and have not been able, in their childish view of life, to understand how the 'good Father' could allow such a thing to happen. As a result, they have felt, at least for a time, much bitterness and disappointment. But, later, they have realised the childish character of their reactions, and have been able to alter their outlook. The question is: Why should *this* little girl, in particular, have been so shattered that her whole life was distorted by the experience?

It is certain that the failure of her religious development cannot be put down to any single factor—just as a neurosis, as we have already seen, cannot be traced to a single shock. But, in the above account, we have sought to throw light upon a conjunction of events which is immediately evident. However, we are here given an opportunity to raise a few important points of principle. According to Dr. Hoff—an authority on the psychotherapeutic treatment of young people—a neurosis is characterised by three essential factors: 1. By regression. 2. By the repetition of experiences. 3. By a tendency towards irrational behaviour. It will clarify the position if we take these three points in a different order, in each case considering their influence upon the religious attitude of the patient.

*   *   *   *   *

The tendency towards irrational behaviour. The patient does all sorts of meaningless things, under a compulsion to do them, although he knows they are absurd. Our neurotic young woman commits one meaningless act after the other, but cannot stop the process. Of course, these acts had an *inner* meaning, as the reader knows, but we regard an act as meaningless if the patient is not aware of its cause and purpose. No one is likely to assert for example that the patient went to prison of set purpose. When this happened, it was 'a bit of bad luck,' and was felt to be doubly tragic, since it was, as she saw it, incomprehensible. In like manner, the confirmed alcoholic knows that he is ruining his life, but that does not stop him; and since he does not understand *why* he drinks, he regards his self-destruction as something arbitrary and meaningless, just as our patient does.

But, when we penetrate the minds of such cases and dig down to the subconscious urges and purposes, we discover a number of links forming a chain; what seemed meaningless is revealed as a complete logical process. Our patient cherished, below the level of consciousness, a very strong hatred for her mother—so strong in fact that it could not completely be held down and, in part, forced its way into consciousness.

There can be no doubt that in the human mind there exists a centre where moral judgments are formed, and this centre does not permit hatred of the mother. But our patient was not able to master her hatred and thus she was condemned by her own inner judgment. She experienced a strong feeling of guilt. But guilt calls for expiation. Guilt that is known to the conscious mind can be expiated consciously. Unconscious guilt cries out for expiation too; on a level unknown to the conscious mind, it demands punishment and atonement. Seen from this angle the strange story of our patient is easily understood. Her persistent tendency towards self-destruction was derived from an unceasing urge towards self-punishment. Her hatred of her mother was boundless. The punishment must accordingly be immeasurably great. She yearned in the depths of her mind for more and more punishment, and lost no time in imposing it upon herself. We must not overlook the fact that, when questioned by the police, she at once confessed not only to crimes she had committed, but to others of which she was *innocent*. It is true that she robbed others; but this was nothing compared with the way in which she robbed herself. At the mercy of the force operating from the subconscious level, she deprived herself of everything. Her sense of guilt never ceased to drive her downhill. This is the *irrationalism* of which we have spoken; yet it is, in truth, perfectly rational and logical. It seems irrational only when the underlying causes are hidden.

In the patient's attitude towards religion we note the same seeming irrationalism. She did not know why she broke away from religion, or why she still hated and rejected it. On the surface, her reactions made no sense. Yet all becomes clear when we get down to her underlying principle of conduct: *I am going to let you all down!* Unconsciously she wants to leave God, also, in the lurch; and, since God is on the highest level, she has no option but to sink to the lowest level. At the same time, she is, without realising it, seeking liberation from the sense of guilt towards God caused—as she realised later—by the fact that her aggressive attitude towards life was also directed against God. When she went on the street her sense of guilt, as we should expect, suffered a further increase, followed by a still stronger yearning for punishment. In her religious experience, she was caught up in a vicious circle revolving around fixed points: rejection of God, hatred, self-punishment, and the necessary absence of atonement and salvation. Every turn of the circle intensified the pressure. This brings us to the second of the above mentioned three points.

Repetition of Experience. In spite of the dramatic character of the events linked with the death of the father and her development as a child, the patient's history is *not*, in a formal sense, a real drama, for that demands dynamic energy urging the action forward.

What we find, in this case, is a repetition of the same thing in different fields of life. There is no new tendency. The whole neurotic pattern pivots about two points: the experience of having been let down, and the determination to make others suffer in the same way. In her home, in her marriage, towards her children, in her profession, and towards herself: it was always the same. The patient was completely tied to a specific pattern of action which she was forced to repeat; she was, as the psychoanalysts say, the victim of a *fixation*. Twice, and each time in the same fashion, she threw away a good position. The repetitive character of the neurosis is seen here with particular clarity. Let us look more closely at these two events.

Quite suddenly, she had the feeling that she must—like her father—take her own life. She journeyed into the country to be quite undisturbed for the act. At the last moment, she was overcome by some inhibition which stopped her actually committing suicide. But she had left her post without permission and felt she could not return. The second time was a repetition of the first, except that she embezzled money, and it was impossible for her to return. We do not think it would be possible to find a more convincing demonstration of the manner in which experiences affecting the subconscious are repeated later in the form of symptoms.

In her religious life, also, we discover the same repetition of experience. When, later on, the patient improved under treatment and became more accessible to religious influences, she told the doctor, quite spontaneously, that she always saw in her mind, 'the God who had taken away her father.' Her mode of experiencing religious matters was very tendencious: she was particularly interested in events that seemed to demonstrate the 'cruelty of God,' and firmly retained such things in her mind. She ignored completely everything which illustrated the goodness and grace of God, and when asked—while under treatment—to mention examples of this aspect of God, she could not point to a single thing although she tried to do so. We see that the neurotic pattern effective in the religious field also; it ensures that the original experience, 'the bad God,' so far from fading away, will be kept fresh in her mind and even strengthened. Her inner conflict and her religious attitude are both fixed in a rigid pattern.

This disposes of the question raised above; why do *other* children, who have suffered similar experiences, not show similar symptoms? The neurotic sufferer cannot transcend an experience like a normal person; this girl had not the capacity to outgrow what had happened to her. She clung to her childhood emotions and allowed them to colour subsequent events. God remained always for her the same God who had so disappointed her. This leads us to the third point:

Regression. It is already clear that the patient shows a marked tendency to return to childhood. Indeed her whole attitude is infantile. She did not master life; but expected life to look after her. These are all characteristic symptoms of the well-known phenomenon of regression. She clings desperately to the emotional states of childhood and repeats them over and over again. Despite all her worldly experience, she remains fundamentally infantile in the most naive sense of the term—not least in abandoning her responsibilities and placing herself in the arms of the state—a father-substitute, needless to say. Regression is equally manifest in the religious sphere. Freud could not attain to an objective analysis of religion, for he was himself subject to a virtual fixation caused by his profound philosophical prejudices; but we know that he saw in religion nothing more than a neurosis of the regressive type. In his view, religion was thrust upon children by their elders and accepted by them before they could form a true judgment. But if psychic development is normal, the beliefs and commandments taught to the children are thrown off. In the case of neurosis, however, this process of getting rid of religion does not take place, and the subject remains fixed in the state proper only to the undeveloped child, providing an example of a regressive neurosis. A careful examination of the psychological foundations of belief and disbelief makes it clear that Freud was entirely wrong, and that the exact *opposite* of what he described is the truth.

It is true that a state of regression results in the patient retaining childish notions about religion. But these notions have nothing to do with *genuine* religious experience; they represent a neurotic distortion. It would be a gross misunderstanding of the words of Christ: 'Unless you become as little children, you shall not enter into the Kingdom of Heaven' to imagine that a regression to the immature notions of childhood is essential to real religious experience. To become as little children means to be open in heart and receptive, to keep as pure as a child during the period of adolescence. The process of becoming mature is of decisive importance for the religious life; it is then that the crude ideas of childhood must be outgrown, if religious faith is to be strong enough to stand firm amidst the storms of real life. This transcendence of the childish stage is difficult, and it is no accident that so many young people fall away from faith during adolescence, when this process should take place.

Before passing on we would like to urge the reader not to make the mistake of taking for granted—as so many do—the falling away from religious life and faith of large masses of people in our age; not to accept this as if it were decreed by fate. On the contrary, we ought to track down each individual, to find out exactly at what point the faith which he had once, in all probability possessed as a child began to fade out. When we do this we find that many young people turn away from religion long before childhood ends. The reader would be surprised at the apparently wholly unimportant things which play a role in this process. Perhaps it should be mentioned, at this point, that we are now engaged in compiling a list of the precise causes of loss of faith in individual cases. This will be published; and will form our special contribution to the problem of spiritual guidance in the present-day. The priest himself must decide to what extent he will make use of this study. The majority, however, suffer loss of faith during the stormy days of puberty. The proportion who tain to maturity in religion, as well as in a biological sense, is latively small. Many reject religion openly and consciously. ut the majority return, in a neurotic regression, to the naive otions of childhood, and fail to develop further. This, in its urn, gives rise to two possibilities: either God is experienced enceforth as the 'good soft-hearted Father in Heaven,' who ermits and forgives everything; or as the God of senseless punish- ient, 'the bad Man' of childish fears. In the case of our patient, we e the operation of the second pattern and we realise, even better an before, why her conception of God never changes. In the ise of both possibilities, the failure to develop on the religious de is the result of a neurotic regression: in the latter case, it results i indignation and rebellion — the real cause of which is not onsciously known; in the first, we find an external faith which no more than a veneer, since it does not rest upon any genuine iterior experience and must wilt away when confronted with ie realities of life.

Faith as such is not regression. Quite the reverse. Genuine faith annot develop unless regression has been overcome. The onsequences of regression in the field of religion are disastrous. he breakdown of true religion is frequently caused by the iechanism of regression.

*   *   *   *   *

If the foregoing be accepted, the work of psychotherapy in learing up neurotic states is seen to be of the utmost significance or the life of faith. Experience teaches us that almost every kind f psychotherapy is, in reality, bound up with changes in the ttitude of the mind towards religious matters. At the same time, t would be a profound mistake to assume that the psychotherapist cts with a religious purpose in view. He must be concerned vith the health of his patient and with nothing else. If he is himself . religious man, he will, in his private capacity, be glad if side-by- ide with the therapy, he can feel he is contributing something

towards the care of souls. It would not be in accordance wit
his principles as a therapist to discuss religion with his patient
for this would be to transgress the proper bounds of the medic
field; and if he did, it would constitute a kind of *medical* spiritu
direction, to which strong objection must be taken. The patien
must take upon himself to draw the conclusions which result from
the removal of irrational tendencies, repetition, and regression
or, as the case may be, discuss them with a priest. This proces
(spiritual re-education, as we might perhaps call it) is exceedingl
slow, difficult and complicated, and it would be impossible t
overemphasise the need for tact and caution. To attempt to g
too quickly, to say prematurely: 'You *must* do this, or that
can undo all the good achieved and block the path to furthe
progress. The priest must not forget, in this connection, tha
while we take the standpoint of the Church as a matter of cours
it is very far from being so to a traveller along the road leadin
to faith. Too much must not be expected from one who is jus
beginning to find his way.

To give a concrete example we will return to our patien
Not only were her symptoms very serious but she received treat
ment far too late. Nevertheless, when she experienced th
phenomenon of transference, the repetition of the child-fathe
relationship with the psychotherapist, which she even correcte
in part, there came into being, suddenly and quite spontaneously
an interest in religion. The reader who has understood the relation
ships indicated in the foregoing will not be surprised at this. Th
next step was that she expressed, quite independently, a desir
to go to Church. Each time she went she came back full of problem
of the interior life. She is now struggling with these, and it woul
be unwise to assume too easy a victory; there will no doubt b
many backslidings. But she is a step further. She does not turn
away from God; she is seeking to reach an understanding wit
Him. She is still far removed from religion as taught by th
Church, and she still rejects the priest as representative of th

Church. (We would like to remark, in passing, that the methods adopted by priests in dealing with persons seeking their way back to the Church, slowly and in the face of many difficulties, require special tact and delicate psychological insight. Brenninkmeyer (2 a) points out, rightly, that priests often increase the difficulties of the seeker by talking as if from the pulpit; they teach objective truth and pay no attention to the subjective situation of the individual). The main point, however, is that, after long years of complete stagnation, *things are moving*, a dynamic process has started and we have to await its further development. She has begun suddenly to attend the May devotions. It is possible that this is an indication of her line of progress. Her totally embittered relationship to her mother is being slowly altered under the influence of the psychotherapeutic treatment. Mary, the Mother of Heaven, has come within her field of vision; and perhaps, finally, she may become conscious of the Church as Mother.

*　　*　　*　　*　　*

Our second case-history is concerned with a man at the height of his powers. After much hesitation he feels he must consult a doctor. His symptoms are of no definite character; he cannot even describe them clearly. He complains of fatigue, believes he has lost initiative, that he is getting less and less able to do his work; he suffers from a feeling of inferiority, his career is as good as over, he has not achieved anything like what he could have done, now there is nothing to look forward to, he is faced with decline. The patient, who is a professor, exhibits strong symptoms of uneasiness which he is unable to explain. 'Formerly,' he says, 'I occupied a position in the centre of life, now I stand on its fringe.' Asked about his personal relationships he describes them as 'perfectly all right.' He has no conflicts; he lives very happily with his mother; he never wanted to marry, because he could not leave his mother, who has nobody but him. He has never had any extra-marital relations, because such would be against his religion.

It was a long time before he discovered, while undergoin therapeutic treatment, the reason for his mysterious uneasines The truth was revealed, for the most part, through a dream. Freu was well justified in describing dreams as 'the high-road to th subconscious.' In the following pages, and especially in the nex chapter, we will furnish clear proofs of this fact. The patien dreamed that he had to bathe in the Danube; but he found th water too cold, and he refused. He said he would bathe in warm water. Then, suddenly, he saw in front of him a man in bathin trunks, and identified him as General Eisenhower. Accordin to the well-known method, the patient was then asked wh associations were suggested to his mind by the events in the drean It then transpired that his mother had often taken him to the banl of the Danube when he was a child; but he never liked goin and felt a strong sensation of uneasiness when he did. To th question as to associations of 'warm water' he hesitated a long tim and then came out suddenly with: 'There is a popular expressior "a warm man," meaning a homosexual.' The almost naked ma fits in to this interpretation. The meaning of Eisenhower remaine long unfathomable. Finally, the solution was found in the fac that the patient's father had been a railway man (Eisenbahner). Ther had occurred in the dream one of those disarrangements to whic Freud refers; Eisenbahner was transformed into Eisenhower We can hardly doubt that the general represented a father figure

This dream makes it quite clear that the patient has a homosexua tendency, hitherto not manifested. It remained latent and wa not consciously realised by the patient, although he had, fron time to time, very strong desires and phantasies of this nature all of which were thrust back into the unconscious as being improper Establishing themselves there, they despatched messages to th conscious level in the form of the mysterious symptoms whicl drove the patient to the doctor in the first instance. All th symptoms were symbols of the conflict taking place within hi mind. Let us look at some of them: 'I feel myself inhibited and uneasy,' this is as much as to say: 'I have to be continually thrusting feelings down and imposing checks on myself'; 'I am inferior,' in other words: 'I am abnormal.' 'My career is over,' in other words: 'I am guilty and must suffer punishment with loss of position.' We must not forget that, for the subconscious mind, desires are the equivalent of actual deeds. The real motive for his lack of interest in the opposite sex is now obvious. It was not due to devotion to his mother nor to religion; but to his sexual aberration.

It is not long since sexual perversion was looked upon as an inborn characteristic. Accordingly, the sufferer felt himself free from responsibility, and doctors felt themselves to be in the same position—they could not possibly do anything about it. But modern developments in the psychology of the subconscious have created quite a new outlook. We now know that defects *in psychic development* play a decisive rôle in the problem, the perversion itself being, in many cases, no more than a symptom. On the other hand, however, we must not deceive ourselves. An ordinary neurosis presents a serious therapeutic problem; but perversion ranks as more difficult to cure than almost any other psychic disorder. We must avoid expressing false optimism and must not promise more than we can perform.

When we examine the life of our patient more closely, we at once discover a factor of decisive significance; his parents were divorced while he was still in the womb. His father disappeared before he was born. The child spent his early years alone with his mother. Here, again, at the risk of repetition, we pause to point out the absolutely central importance of a healthy family life—a point which can never be overstressed. The absence of the other parent caused the small boy to cling all the more to the mother, unaware of the existence of a father. When the child was four, the mother received news which made her weep; she put on black clothes and took her child with her to a funeral. Now, for the first time, our patient discovered that he had, or *had*

had, a father. This fact profoundly affected the child. How deep was the impression is witnessed by a dream which the patient related during his treatment: he sits by the side of the driver in a motor car, when he suddenly feels that he has no *right* to sit there, that the place belongs to someone else. He wants to jump out at once although the car is going very fast. The patient, when questioned, immediately connected this dream with the journey he and his mother made to the burial of the father. The parallel is fairly obvious: he had, up to then, occupied a place by the side of his mother without knowing that it really belonged to someone else. But suddenly he found out that it did and wished at once to vacate the place and make room for the other. But it was too late. His father was dead. The course of events forced upon the small boy a feeling of guilt, while no opportunity existed for making restitution. The child's subjective reaction was, roughly: I am occupying a place to which I am not entitled. Later on, this situation, which existed in relation to his mother, was transferred to *all* women. He erected a barrier to separate him from his natural sex instinct. It is interesting to note, in this connection, that, even as a middle-aged man, he retained a vivid recollection of an unimportant detail in the journey to his father's burial: the car in which he sat with his mother sought to pass quickly over a railway crossing; then the gate was closed and they were forced to a lengthy wait. Why did the patient remember so well this unimportant event? This was no accident; it was another example of tendencious apperception, in the sense of Alfred Adler. The event in question corresponded with experience so exactly that he never forgot it. In his life a gate was suddenly closed, a barrier was set up, when he was overwhelmed by the feeling that he was not entitled to his position in relation to his mother.

This inhibition was later to go with him in every contact with women; he was to remain fixed in this subjective experience and to repeat it continually. (cf. the note to the first case-history). This fixation and the event leading to it were symbolised by the

ailway-crossing incident; and, also, by a curious fact related by the
atient, namely that, after the burial, his favourite game as a
hild was one he called 'barriers.' With his little building bricks,
e constructed railway-crossings and, when in the country, he cut
ranches, arranged them across a path, and pretended they were
vel-crossing barriers. Needless to say, all this was an expression
f the deep inhibition he carried in his mind. Such a case helps us
o see clearly that even the smallest things are full of meaning, if
nly we know the relationships. A fact of immense significance
or the priest.

The manner in which the patient clung to his mother in later
fe illustrates the irrational tendency dominating him—a tendency
ery characteristic of such cases. One would certainly think that
is infantile situation would prompt him to break away from his
other later in life. Not at all. On the contrary, he made a point,
uite consciously, of carefully looking after her, although, in the
nconscious, he must have felt a strong grievance against her,
r she had failed to hold the father (cf. the first case), and had
ver even spoken to him of his existence. The patient did
ccasionally indulge in outbursts of anger against his mother,
d when, during treatment, he was asked what caused these,
explained that she made too many claims upon him and tied
m to her apron strings. We see that he placed the blame upon
factor that was not the primary cause, but a secondary *result*
the original cause of which the patient was unaware.

There can be no doubt that the patient suffers from an unconscious
eling of guilt towards his father, whose proper place he had taken,
cording to his own subjective experience. But he can find no
ay of liberating himself from this guilt, for he does not know the
use, and he is compelled to go on in the situation that gave rise
his trouble; in other words, to remain with his mother and thus
tensify his unconscious guilt complex. Meanwhile, his dreams
ntinue to indicate that the father problem stands at the centre
his difficulty. Again and again, he dreams of travelling in a

railway-train that is de-railed. His father—as the reader knows—
was a railway-man, and the dream symbolises the fact that, through
the re-emergence of his father, the patient became de-railed, and
found himself travelling along the wrong track—namely the path
of his latent homosexuality. The inhibition as to women is given
an unconscious expression, and, in the same way, there develops
an urge towards the male sex, which, considered fundamentally
signifies neither more nor less than the desire to find his father
and through him find liberation from guilt.

We know very well that such a sketch as the foregoing does
no more than give a bare outline of the relationships in question.
We know also that we have followed up only one track out
of all the many psychic developments which take place in the
mind of a single human being. But, on the other hand, no one
who appreciates the logical pattern in the foregoing will be able
to maintain that we are dealing with purely theoretical constructions,
with interpretations incapable of proof that have been imported
into the case without the patient himself being able to do anything
about it. To the patient these things are intensely real. To the
priest, also, they are real.

It is possible that the priest who accepts the conclusions we
have drawn may nevertheless ask the question: Would it not be
better to let these things stay where they are, instead of dragging
them up from the subconscious regions? As a matter of fact, it is
not infrequently the case that harm is done by too much stirring
up of the depths. But the priest will quickly change his mind when
he learns how great was the influence of the 'dragging up' process
upon the religious life of the patient. It has already been explained
that he gave a wrong reason for his indifferent attitude toward
the opposite sex. He attributed it to a desire to follow the teaching
of the Church which does not permit extra-marital relations. To
this one may reply: why then did he not marry? It would be hard
to avoid the rational conclusion that the patient is misusing religion
as a screen for his neurosis, calling upon the commandments

explain actions based, in reality, upon the neurotic tendencies which grip him and will not let him go. Possibly the priest will not allow himself to be convinced by this reference to a false religious attitude. He may say: 'Very good—Yes, he does misuse religion, but the chief thing is that he lives according to its teachings.'

This is not so. Educated in a strongly religious atmosphere, he remained faithful to the Church in childhood and youth; he was looked upon in his parish as a sincere, even a model, Catholic. But behind the façade, things were very different. From year to year the inhibition which so dominated his life made itself felt increasingly in the religious field. It became more and more difficult for him to receive the sacraments, a state of things which puzzled him, for he felt that, rationally, he was full of reverence for the Church and its eternal laws and happy to be a Catholic. After confession, he no longer experienced the accustomed feeling of relief (from a supernatural standpoint this plays no part in the matter, needless to say; but is nevertheless of practical importance, since cases of this sort are often no more to be persuaded to receive the sacraments). Only after much hesitation and severe inward struggles could he manage to go again to confession. This went on for years; he felt ashamed to face his confessor, in view of his infrequent visits to the confessional, and finally gave up going to him but went now and then to a strange priest, when his chief idea was to get it over quickly and, above all, to avoid any personal contact. At the end of this wearisome pilgrimage he found himself faced with complete religious emptiness and he no longer took the sacraments. Occasionally, on a Sunday, he would wander into some Church, only to experience divided feelings.

In this case, also, it was found possible to trace the causes leading to loss of faith; to show how the divine seed was increasingly driven out by weeds. A neurosis gradually damages the natural psychic foundations which should serve the purpose of helping the individual to a fuller and richer co-operation with the life of grace. The patient is inhibited in his religious life and cannot develop; in the long run, he sinks into a state of religious apathy. This failure is determined by the fact that he suffers from an illness and needs a cure on the natural level, a task for medicine and not for religion.

As a contrast, we will now outline, very briefly, another case within our experience. A young woman who was brought up along definitely anti-religious lines and later in life showed complete indifference towards religion, began, quite suddenly, to develop a keen interest for everything connected with religion, eagerly sought out the company of priests and became, in fact, quite excessively pious. Then she disappeared for several months and, on returning home, she manifested—as before—nothing but indifference to religion. An examination of the case conducted at a later date threw light on this strange affair: the patient was manifestly homosexual and, in the course of her quest for a suitable partner, had come to know an elderly lady who was very religious and did not want to have anything to do with her advances. In order to make an impression upon her and convince her of the genuineness of her feelings—and very likely also through a process of identification—the patient turned her mind to religion, while, at the same time, showering presents upon the elderly lady. This proved an expensive matter, and to obtain money, the patient committed a robbery, was discovered, and spent some time in prison. When she was set free, she lost interest in the elderly lady. She sought out other partners, and as they were not religious her efforts to appear religious became superfluous.

Here we note two opposite types of development. In the one case, a neurotic tendency, homosexuality, leads apparently to religion; in the other, the same tendency destroys the life of faith. Yet it is readily seen that these two cases possess a common factor of importance: a neurotic tendency forms a serious obstacle to the development of religious life. Faith which rests upon neurosis, or is influenced by it, is never well-founded and genuine.

*   *   *   *   *

We draw near the end of this chapter, which should have made it clear that our conclusions, notwithstanding the cautious manner in which they have been presented, are of central significance for the priest, and for the direction of souls in general. At present, we are far from realising the far-reaching importance of these modern methods, destined, as they are, to bring about a decisive advance in our whole approach to the care of souls.

To sum up: *in the life of faith, no less than in the life of the body, a maturing process is essential.* The religious life in fact represents such a process: one does not *have* faith, one *wins* it afresh every day. A dynamic forward movement is vital if faith is to remain a living thing. This movement rests upon the dynamic development of the personality as a whole. We believe ourselves to be the first to examine the decline of faith in the light of actual case-histories of psychic illness, thereby underlining the significance of psychic dynamism, activity, and continual development of the personality in its essential nature. Some beginnings were made by Kierkegaard (*Die Krankheit zum Tode*: Diederichs, Jena, 1938), when he spoke of the necessity of metamorphosis in the life of faith. More recently, B. Kihn has put forward views which may, perhaps, be interpreted in this sense. He says: 'A metaphysically acceptable and successful inward development presupposes that the *urge towards faith*, in other fields, is adequately extended and consolidated. Only then will it be capable of supporting the metaphysical edifice.'

In the introductory part of this study we spoke of the harmonious view of the world in which the lower places itself at the disposal of the higher; but this harmony is not possible without the *active co-operation* of the lower. This process plays a decisive part within the framework of human personality. Here, too, the subordination of the lower to the higher is an essential condition for the establishment of inner harmony. Here, again, we see that the 'lower'—for example sexuality—is not to be rejected in itself; on the contrary, it may be accepted *positively*, bearing in mind that it must be subordinate to the higher.

This harmony is the foundation for conscious free decisions, giving rise to creative personal acts, which, as we saw, support the life of super-nature and allow it to fulfil its works. Thus, what Kihn calls the 'urge to faith' and what we call the dynamic of faith, is to be understood as the *result* of the harmonious development of personality. The manner in which neurosis makes this harmony impossible has been adequately demonstrated and proved. A well ordered state is replaced by an ataxy, whereby the personality becomes torn asunder, uncertain of itself, and subject to oscillations, its separate tendencies warring against one another instead of working in co-operation. Instead of being able to draw support from every portion of his soul, the neurotic sufferer is dominated by a dictatorship exercised by a portion of himself. The hierarchy of the personality—according to which, as G. R. Heyer puts it, each lower stratum of life forms the foundation for a higher stratum, by which the lower is contained and roofed over—is thus destroyed, and with it the psychic dynamic of the soul. What remains is inhibition, stagnation, barriers and regression: in short, the ever revolving vicious circle known to the reader. The door is closed; the road is barred. This brings with it, looking at it from the natural level, the results which we have already described: doubt, failure, decline of faith, or even downright rejection. Soukup (*Geopferte Natur*: 1941), to whose valuable work we have referred more than once, has given a somewhat extended meaning to the saying: *gratia supponit naturam*, in the following terms: 'Grace is built upon a foundation of sacrificed nature.' He means that, 'faith and theology can be perfected only by those who, moved by obedience, confidence and the love of God, are able again and again to sacrifice purely natural and rational knowledge.' Looked at in this fashion we can accept the idea of 'sacrificed nature.' Should it mean, however, that we can afford *to do without natural development*, or even that it should be sacrificed, we are compelled to contradict uch a statement. We believe the opposite of this, namely that a healthy development on the natural level is a preliminary condition of a genuine development of faith; and should feel inclined to put the matter differently; grace is built upon a foundation *of developed nature*.

There are three misunderstandings that must, by all means, be avoided. Firstly, it might be supposed that, once the neurosis has been cured, faith is restored: this cannot be the case, if only for the reason that faith depends upon the grace of God. Secondly, some readers may perhaps think that because we have traced a connection between neurosis and the failure of religious life, that every such failure is due to some kind of neurosis. But this would not correspond to our interpretation of the problem, because we firmly hold that a man can of his own free will—in the absence of neurotic compulsion—decide against faith in God. But we also believe that a considerable proportion of those who fall away from religion *are* driven by a neurotic mechanism. To give a definite estimate is not, of course, possible; a widespread investigation carried out over a very wide field and including a separate examination of each particular case, would be required, before any attempt of this kind would be justified. In the third place it is clearly to be understood that in all these cases what is demonstrated is simply that the *outward form* of religious life or practice breaks down. Nothing is proved as to the interior life of faith in this manner. Nevertheless, it would appear to us that the symptomatology, even if it is the outward only that is in question, is so alarming that we should, in the future, pay every possible attention to this problem. We have spoken of a closed door which bars the way to dynamic development for the neurotic. Bishop Fulton Sheen, from the standpoint of the spiritual director, makes use of a similar comparison when he speaks of a *prison*, and of psychotherapy as the file which can aid the prisoner to escape. We are reminded of the striking saying of Ferdinand Birnbaum: 'The doors of the neurotic hell are locked from *inside*.' Only from within can they be opened; the patient himself has to use the key. This has the further significance that under all circumstances, the patient must retain the *possibility* of opening the doors; and with it, the *responsibility* for using the key. In almost all cases, however, this liberation will succeed only with the aid of a psychotherapist. For this reason, and also because of the great importance of psychotherapy for the religious life we pointed out in an earlier publication (*Seelsorge und Neurose* 1951), that, in our opinion, a neurotic case is bound in *duty*—otherwise he commits a sin—to place himself under treatment. But as we know, the psychotherapist cannot open the door of the prison. He can do no more than help the patient to find the key.

But there is One who can do all things. For the omnipotent God there are no obstacles; with Him nothing is impossible. He can open *every* door, from without or from within. We are not unaware of the fact that our explanation—despite every attempt at clarity—might possibly give rise to the impression that we stand for some kind of psychologism. The truth is that we, more than others, see a grave danger in psychologism; for the logical upshot of this line of thought is to derive all supernatural things from nature alone. For this reason, we cannot lay too much stress upon the omnipotence of God. In the field of pure science we are, of course, bound to proceed along rational lines.

For the priest, the position is different: we most earnestly urge him not to rely *passively* upon the omnipotence and grace of God, but, armed with all the weapons of modern knowledge, to *make active use* of every known means of *preparing the path for the operation of grace in the world of nature.* In order to underline still further the convictions we hold on this matter we will quote again from Thomas Aquinas: 'God is able to lift up every one of his creatures to a higher level of reality than that to which it is raised by natural forces.'

When this book appeared for the first time in Vienna, the Holy Father had not yet delivered his important speech to the Congress of Psychotherapy.

We may here quote a few sentences from this address:

'We should certainly not find fault with depth psychology if it deals with the psychic aspect of religious phenomena and endeavours to analyze and reduce it to a scientific system, even if this research is new and if its terminology is not found in the past. We mention this last point, because misunderstandings can easily arise when psychology attributes new meanings to already accepted expressions. Prudence and reserve are needed on both sides in order to avoid false interpretations and to make it possible to reach a reciprocal understanding.

It pertains to the technique of your science to clarify the questions of the existence, the structure, and the mode of action of this dynamism. If its outcome proves to be positive, it should not be declared irreconcilable with reason or faith. This would only show that, even in its deepest roots, "esse ab alio" also implies an "esse ad alium," and that St. Augustine's words: "Fecisti nos ad te; et inquietum est cor nostrum donec requiescat in te" find a new confirmation in the very depth of the psychic being. Even if there were question of a dynamism involving all men, peoples, epochs, and cultures, what a help and what an invaluable help this would be for the search after God and the affirmation of His existence!' We are justified in regarding these expressions, coming from the highest quarter, as an encouragement to future research along the lines indicated.

CHAPTER V.

A CASE OF ACUTE HYSTERIA WITH ITS
ANALYSIS AND CURE

THE TWO FORMS of clearly marked neurosis most often met with
by the priest and liable to give him the most trouble are *acute
hysteria* and the so-called *obsessional* neurosis. In addition, we
might mention the phobias; fear of open spaces, fear of bacteria
etc., which may also be reckoned to the compulsory neurosis,
characterised as we have explained by compulsory irrational
patterns. It is with the above two forms, however, that we propose
to occupy ourselves in the next two chapters. At the same time,
we must mention that today various separate neurotic tendencies,
such as neurotic debility, may cause trouble to the priest in an
equal degree; but we cannot, within this frame-work, take
them up in detail and would refer the reader to the excellent,
practically very useful work of Brenninkmeyer (12 a).

Both of these disorders constitute a serious danger to the religious
life. Hysteria is, in addition, a source of *personal* danger to the
priest. The following instructive cases will make it clear how
a priest can run into danger; how he can guard against it; and,
finally, in what manner hysteria affects religious life.

A man aged between thirty and forty arrived at a doctor's
house in a state of great excitement, accompanied by his young
wife. The day before—he told the doctor—his wife came home
in a dazed condition; she spoke as if her mind were confused;
she seemed to be trying to tell him that she had been raped by the
priest in his presbytery. The husband went to the presbytery
and found out that his wife has actually been there, and further,
that the room where he was received was as described by his wife.
Now—the husband continued—he did not know what to think.
On the one hand, he was compelled to feel that his wife was in

n irresponsible state, and that he could not rely on what she told im and, further, the priest, who denied very emphatically the harge brought against him, gave him a feeling of confidence. On the other hand, it was a fact that his wife had actually remained or some considerable time in the priest's house. He had tried to alk her out of it,' but the only result was increased confusion.

The husband implored the doctor to clear the matter up, for is wife's sake as well as his own. The diagnosis was 'dazed ondition due to hysteria,' and the young woman was sent to hospital for mental and nervous cases.

There her life-history and background were examined in detail. The patient had been married for some years; she described her married life as 'completely satisfactory'; no differences of any kind, not even the smallest, existed between the pair. This statement seemed to be corroborated by a superficial examination of the position: the two were much attached and seemed to be in the closest unity. It transpired that a few days before the above mentioned event the patient underwent some kind of psychic alteration. Following upon the visit of a family of friends, she began to suffer from sleeplessness, and felt herself inwardly disturbed and excited. She admitted not 'getting on' well with the wife of the friend. She made up her mind to consult the family doctor. On the way, she experienced strange sensations; a burning spread over her whole body and was especially noticeable in the palms of the hands; she believed herself to be *stigmatised*, and was convinced she would never get rid of the marks. She was told by the doctor that there was nothing serious and given a sedative, which she took. She then went to see the priest to settle some business about the church tax, with which she was in arrears. As to what then followed, she could recollect it only in a dream-like fashion and did not seem sure herself as to what was reality and what imagination. She suddenly felt unwell and extremely tired; the priest brought her into another room and let her lie down on a sofa. He talked to her and expressed sympathy for her that she had no child and was sexually unsatisfied; finally he took advantage of her. She was able to remember that, at a particular moment, she experienced a marvellous feeling of relief.

The next stage was a further analysis under a narcotic; the patient received an injection of sodium pentotal—the so-called truth drug —a name by no means appropriate since this drug, while helping to bring to light unconscious conflicts, does not compel the patient to reveal anything he seeks to keep back. The use of this drug in cases of judicial examination is to be rejected most decisively; it is permissible solely when indicated by a doctor as an aid to clearing up unconscious conflicts, that is purely on medical grounds and even then it must be employed with the greatest caution. In view of the difficult nature of the case, we need hardly add that the analysis under the narcotic was carried out in the presence of a witness.

The analysis did not at first yield any notable results. The patient repeated what she had previously said. But just as she was beginning to get sleepy she asserted in a clear emphatic voice, repeating each sentence several times, 'I wanted to deceive my husband; my *dearest wish* was to deceive him.' She then slept a while; and when awakening, became very talkative, illustrating the cathartic effect of this form of treatment; but it was noteworthy that, notwithstanding the stream of words uttered, there was no reference to her husband, and when the doctors turned the conversation in his direction she went off at a tangent. The significance of this analysis is obvious; there was no question of her having been raped. Her story of what took place represented a *wish-fulfilment*—the expression of a subconscious wish to deceive her husband.

The further elucidation of this interesting case is closely linked to events in the earlier life of the patient.

When Germany was occupied in 1945, she found herself in imminent danger of being raped but it did not come to the ultimate act. At a rather later date, she carried on an affair with

n officer of the occupying forces quartered in her home. This
vent on for some time, when it transpired that the officer was
narried. He was recalled, promising to keep in touch with her;
ut she never heard anything more of him.

The patient gave her husband an ingeniously distorted version
f these events. It was true (she said) that she had had intercourse
vith a man before she met him; but it was a case of being raped.
The relationship with the officer was not mentioned, while the
near-rape, which had really taken place, was now put forward
s real rape.

This presentation of her position was by no means accidental.
Side-by-side with an easily understood desire to cast a veil over
certain portions of her history, we note that the mechanism of
hysteria plays a vital part. In her early days, before any of the
foregoing events took place, the patient was torn in two by a
severe conflict. On the one hand, she felt a strong urge towards
sexual intercourse; while, on the other, she felt an equally strong
moral inhibition: 'Thou shalt not!' In passing, we note that some
such conflict is experienced by all young people as they reach
maturity; but with neurotics the natural factors are mingled with
pathological motives which, as we shall see later, make the conflicts
peculiarly difficult and often insoluble. Under the pressure of these
conflicts and difficulties the patient—as she herself admitted later—
took refuge in an imaginary notion of being raped. For *rape*, and
that alone, seemed able to solve her problem by satisfying both
the warring tendencies; it gave the opportunity of sexual intercourse while liberating her from moral responsibility. Who could
blame her when she was not acting as a free agent and did not
consciously give consent? In this connection we should like to
repeat that what is unconscious cannot be sinful, for sin is possible
only when there is clear knowledge and free will and thoughts
and wishes known to be sinful are given acceptance. If, in psychotherapeutic treatment, something unconscious becomes conscious
and the patient then freely accepts it, knowing it as sinful, then

we obtain the conditions of real sin. True, in the case of the attempted rape the patient offered resistance with success; but the subconscious desire manifested itself later when she converted the attempt into a *real* rape. Thus we have already discovered one cause for the subsequent story she invented, when in a state of hysteria, about her having been raped.

We know that the patient, later on, entered into a liaison with an officer. We cannot doubt that it was very difficult for her to overcome the voice of conscience which was, we know, active in her mind. For this reason she had a *powerful sense of guilt*, which increased after she knew her lover was married; this had, however, nothing to do with genuine repentance. In passing, we must note that this example shows us that the guilt feelings of the neurotic are not compelled to be morbid in all cases, but that, together with disordered sensations of guilt not founded in real guilt, we may find others based upon real guilt. We need hardly explain that the way to remove this real guilt lies outside the scope of pure psychology. 'As every Christian knows, it consists in contrition and sacramental absolution by the priest,' as Pius XII said. It is thus clear how heavy is the responsibility of the psychotherapist in calling upon priestly aid. It was characteristic that she turned for advice to her foster-mother and asked her if this relationship was permissible. Attempts of this sort to find exculpation through others are common; a circumstance which throws a strong light upon the responsibility of the person from whom advice is sought. Her foster-mother assured her that she did nothing wrong; she must not be so stupid as to let her youth slip by without enjoying it. The consequence was that the patient entered into her liaison, but, at the same time, began to have a feeling of secret resentment against her adviser, because she felt that she had led her astray.

To her husband, as we know, she falsified her whole history and never told him anything about her liaison. This could have only one consequence; the feeling of guilt which already existed grew stronger. She had lied to her husband. The typical reaction towards those we have deceived is twofold; on the one hand, we feel a sense of *duty* towards them; but, on the other, there results, often unconsciously, and from the sense of duty, a feeling of *resentment*. In point of fact, the patient (as we shall see) had two feelings in respect of her husband; an exaggerated attachment, and a definite feeling of hatred.

Two tendencies may now be regarded as established in this case: the patient had a feeling of guilt in relation to her husband, and at the same time a strong sensation of resentment. It is not difficult to discover how both of these tendencies were satisfied by her state of confusion and hysteria.

While in this state she experienced, in imagination, an act of rape. This recalled, in twofold fashion, certain past events. Firstly the attempted but resisted rape; and, secondly, the lies which she had told her husband. Here again we see the urge to *repetition*, to experience over again the original shock incident. When she returned to her husband after the visit to the doctor and the priest, and while still in a state of confusion and mental fog, she at once said to him: 'I told you lies before. I was never raped. I had a liaison.' The significance of this was, although the words were not actually spoken: 'Then I was *not* raped, but *now* I was!' Here we can perceive a cathartic process, an attempted purification; the patient has an inner need to confess to her husband. But she is not strong enough to do this, without some kind of external support. She needs to have the experience and to be able to say: 'what I told you before was not true, but *now I have really had the experience I then invented.*' It thus becomes obvious that her state of hysteria brings about a fulfilment of her first inner urge. Now she can confess her guilt and, at the same time, soften down the crudity of her previous untruthfulness by pointing to a genuine experience of the same kind. Along similar lines an explanation is suggested for the peculiar experience she described as 'stigmatisation.' It is an expression of a feeling of guilt, made still clearer by her fear that she would never get rid of the stigmata. It was the hysterical state and the mental confusion that enabled her to confess her guilt and thus cleanse herself. It is scarcely necessary to point out that her second urge—to express resentment against her husband—was also fulfilled through the hysteria; for while in this state she deceived her husband.

We are now in a position to take the analysis a step further. We have already stated that sex conflicts—in themselves by no means abnormal—have origins of a pathological nature in neurotic cases, particularly with hysteria. To trace these origins we will now examine the childhood of our patient. She was an *unwanted* and rejected child: her parents lost no time in placing her with strangers, where she remained up to the age of ten. She was much attached to her father, however, and when she returned home was especially glad to be with him. A special father-attachment is, of course, normal with girls. She had a positive dislike for her mother. We note already a tendency towards 'tendencious apperception'; she threw nearly all the blame for her being 'put away,' on her mother's shoulders, and remembered every smallest thing in her childhood which could be used to blacken her mother. At an early age, she realised that her father was habitually unfaithful to her mother. Her attitude was: 'It serves her right.' But, at the same time, she felt disturbed by the situation. She made a habit of overhearing what she could of the sex relationships of her parents during the night. Her feelings were divided; one part of her was excited and attracted; another disgusted and repelled. 'Doesn't mother know,' she would ask herself, 'that father comes to her from the arms of another woman? How can she put up with that?'

It is clear that we are dealing with one of those cases in which —as we saw in Chapter II.—a sex conflict plays a particularly important part. Whatever one may think about Freudian theories, it must be admitted that here we have the precise situation described by Freud as the Oedipus (or Electra) complex: a peculiarly close relationship exists in these cases between the child and the parent of the *opposite* sex, a relationship mistakenly interpreted by the Freudians as predominantly sexual; while the parent of the *same* sex is regarded as a competitor.

Our patient was attached in the highest degree to her father; yet she was doubly disappointed in him, for he not only betrayed her (as she felt) with her mother, but with a number of other women. Thus, in combination with a very strong tie, we find an *ambivalent* state of mind, a situation characteristic of hysteria. Later on, this ambivalent attitude is transferred to all the other personalities and objects entering the life of the patient. We have just seen that her attitude towards sex was ambivalent. She desires, and yet feels a peculiarly powerful inhibition. Ambivalence is to be seen also in the relationship to the foster-mother, who was made use of as a confidante, but was later attacked by the patient on the ground of having misled her. Most decisive of all is the fact that the ambivalent attitude derived from the early father-daughter relationship was afterwards extended to her own husband. On the one hand, he is the strong man who can be leaned upon, who knows everything and will always protect her—the typical father figure; but, on the other, a personality who dominates and crushes her! Later on the analysis brought out clearly to what an extent she resented the mastery her husband had acquired. The patient who began by speaking of her model marriage and its unbroken harmony adopted suddenly a different tone, and in a very excited manner, as if urged by a strong emotional excitement and in a fashion suggesting real hatred, she began to complain about her husband. He sits high above, as if on a throne and lets himself be worshipped, while she has to remain down below in an attitude of humility and reverence. No opinion except his own has any value; the smallest attempt to assert independence is nipped in the bud. He is the complete dictator; he tries to persuade her that what he wants is always what she wants. In a word, the patient is convinced that she is the oppressed and suppressed party.

As an example, the following incident was produced whic took place just before her last birthday. Her husband asked h what she would like, and she replied: 'For one day to take yo place in this household. At the same time you will take mir —just for this one day.' The husband thought he could buy himse out of this demand with a money present; in other ways, also, h conduct was such as to increase the tension between them. Alwa vastly pleased with himself, he said on various occasions to his wif 'Just see if you can find another man like me—anywhere!' H challenged her to make comparisons, either mentally or physicall With such provocations he almost invited her to deceive him. came out during the analysis that in several cases of men she h recently got to know, she had indulged in fanciful ideas along t line: 'Now what would it be like, if——?' It transpired, furthe that on various occasions she had secretly considered divorc In brief, the alleged 'harmonious marriage' was filled with viole tensions and inner conflicts and was on the point of collapse. Tl close connection between her position as a wife, which she fe to be intolerable, and her hysterical illness, is illustrated by anoth event: the illness began, as the reader knows, just after a visit fro a friendly couple. This marriage was in direct contrast to her ow the wife—whom she disliked—was very much in command, an it was natural enough that this made her own so different positic seem peculiarly insufferable. In consequence, her desire to tak some action against her husband was reinforced. We have se that her peculiar hysterical condition offered a partial satisfactio for this urge; and now we see that her resentment sprang, not on from guilt, but also from a continual feeling of subjection an suppression in her marriage, working in conjunction with h ambivalent psychology.

But even now we have not come to the end of all the underlyin desires and urges which can be held responsible for the hysteri The study of a dream, related by the patient while under analysi will take us a stage further: 'I found myself,' she said, 'in a bi city. I saw that it must be Rome. There was a severe drought; for the lord of the city had ordered the water to be cut off. The people longed for water. I went to a large pipe, which stuck up slantwise out of the ground and was within reach of my hand and opened it. A flood of dirty water—rather like rain water—poured out in my direction. I felt great satisfaction and relief. But then I recollected that the ruler of the city had forbidden the use of water, felt afraid and ran off. I felt that I was being followed.'

The patient proffered a number of associations suggested by this dream: Rome is the seat of the Pope, the centre of the Church; the wealth squeezed out of the people by the Church is carried off there. 'But *they won't get any taxes from me!*' Rome is the town where we had planned to go for our honeymoon, but it did not take place. *Water* is necessary if there is not to be a drought; I like washing and my husband sometimes makes that a reproach. *Piping*: the place where we live has no water laid on; this annoys me greatly. The peasants say they can't afford it; but it is more likely that they are too miserly.

Leaving on one side, for the time being, the suggestive passages about her attitude to the Church, to return to them later, we find ourselves with a fairly clear picture. The dream symbolises the patient's marriage. This is indicated, in the first place, by the place to which it took the dreamer—Rome, where the honeymoon should have been enjoyed. The marriage like the honeymoon did not go according to plan. In the marriage, there was a great drought causing thirst: an explanation of this symbol is hardly necessary, and the meaning was corroborated fully by the analysis. The marriage proved sterile, to the great distress of the patient, who passionately desired children, a wish not shared by her husband. What were the factors that brought about this state of things? Who was the ruler of the city, who ordered a drought? It turned out that the family doctor, the same whom she visited just before her attack, had examined her and discovered a uterus 'as thin as a thread of cotton,' and told her she must never venture to bear a child. This gave a severe shock to the patient and it must be recorded that her neurosis was partly due to this statement of the doctors. During the treatment, the patient had another gynaecological examination and was found fully capable of maternity. It is thus clear that the 'city lord,' in the dream was, in the first place, the doctor. We must remember that the subsequent attitude of the patient towards him was very ambivalent and, in addition to the attachment to him which she professed, she cherished a strong resentment caused by his expression of the above opinion. This attitude is important owing to the fact that the patient's visit to the priest, on the day of her crisis, followed close upon her consultation with the doctor. But the city ruler who forbade the use of water also symbolised another person, namely her *husband*, whom she looked upon as a despot, who had more than once replied to her oft-expressed desire for children by saying they could not possibly afford it. In the dream, the peasants said they had not enough money to construct a water supply, while she thought they were too miserly. The patient was passionately anxious for a child. Doctor and husband forbade it; thus she felt strong resentment against both.

Before proceeding with this dream-analysis, we would like to quote two important statements by Niedermeyer from his well-known dictionary of pastoral medicine (*Handbuch der speziellen Pastoralmedizin in sechs Bänden*: Herder, Vienna, 1948-52): 'While it is a mistake on the part of the orthodox Freudians to concentrate one-sidedly upon the sexual aspects of symbols, it would be as bad a mistake to overlook them, and not at least consider them along with other possibilities. In some cases, this approach is just what is needed to put us on the right track, even when the actual subconscious conflict is not in itself sexual.' In the present case we must certainly not overlook a sexual explanation. The pipe which gushed water in Rome is a very obvious sexual symbol, and the water which the patient caused to flow is the semen which was to make her fertile. Thus, in her dream, she fulfilled her long-cherished wish to bear a child. And not *only* in this dream, but earlier in her semi-conscious hysterical state. This statement finds support in the fact that, when the patient was requested to trace associations suggested to her mind by her feeling of satisfaction and relief in the dream, she at once began to speak of her confused hysterical condition: she had experienced a similar feeling of relief, she said, when with the priest, and she associated with this condition the conviction that *she would immediately have a child*. We thus perceive that the hysterical state fulfilled a further essential tendency of the patient's innermost wishes: namely that she gave birth to a child. It is an interesting point that a parallel exists between the dream and the hysterical state. In the former, it was *muddy* water that gushed forth and the patient felt guilty and ran away, because the ruler had forbidden the use of water. This makes it quite clear that what was in question must have been a *forbidden* way of fulfilling her wishes—in other words, she wanted a child but not from her husband. The ruler who represented first the doctor and then the husband, represents in a different connection and in the last resort, the super-ego, in the sense used in psycho-analytical practice, which we may very loosely call the voice of conscience. In her hysterical state, as in the dream, her wishes found fulfilment along forbidden paths. Why, in this particular case, a priest should have been fixed upon is a matter that we will consider and explain later. In any case, her desire to have a child must form a further vital factor causing her hysterical state.

* * * * *

To sum up, we can say that we are not dealing in the event related by the patient with a real experience but, as the analysis made perfectly clear, with delusions due to hysteria. The pressure of powerful unconscious urges which failed to find an outlet, followed the well-known classical lines and the result was a concentration of pent-up forces which enabled intensive desires suddenly to project imaginary images felt by the subject to be real. The patient's state of mental obscurity served to fulfil the following urges—themselves the cause of the mental state: 1. The resentment felt against her husband. 2. The desire to destroy the despotic and omnipotent attitude of the husband. 3. The desire to betray her husband. 4. The urge to liberate herself from the sense of guilt attaching to her deception of her husband. This was why she experienced, or imagined herself to experience, what she had untruthfully related to him. 5. Her strong desire for a child. 6. The resentment she felt towards the Church and its official representatives.

The last point raises the question why she fixed upon a priest, of all people, to be sacrificed to her hysterical imaginings. This happens, as a matter of fact, frequently with hysteria cases and is always to be feared. As Niedermeyer says: 'A priest cannot be too careful in dealing with such cases—it is they who first of all exalt the priest to the skies, and then do their best to compromise him.'

As we have seen, a characteristic of hysteria is the *ambivalent attitude* of the patient. In the present case this was developed, in the first place, towards the father and was then transferred to every other person or thing. There is no doubt—and the analysis confirms it—that this ambivalent outlook was transferred to the field of religion where it was dominant. On the one hand, the patient shewed a hostile attitude towards the Church (cf. her dream about Rome), but, on the other hand she was interested in religion and more open to its influence than she herself seemed to realise. This ambivalence may be regarded as the characteristic reaction of the hysteric in the sphere of religion. Another pointer to ambivalence in the present case, it might be added, is the question of the tax due to the Church. She did not want to pay this, yet we know that she went to the priest with the express object of settling the matter, of paying at least a part of it. This gives us yet another factor which almost certainly played some part in ringing on the attack of hysteria. As a rule the patient was herself aware of only one of the two tendencies, the other remaining below the level of consciousness and in this way exerting a greater influence. Thus, in the case of our patient, we perceive that the rejection of religion occupied her conscious mind, while there existed in the subconscious a strong tendency towards religion, as was seen during the analysis. In other cases, we find that the tendency towards religion is prominent in the upper levels of the mind, while the other factor in the ambivalence, the hostility towards religion, slumbers in the lower levels, ready, when prompted, to emerge and turn the whole personality away from religion. A small error of tact or a social blunder may arouse a sense of injured dignity; some offence against the subject's feeling for beauty or good taste, or the failure to fulfil some wish—even an unspoken wish—or a hundred other things may turn the mind away. Often the merest trifles sway the whole personality in the religious field. The explanation is that down in the subconscious levels of the mind there *already* exists a feeling against the Christian life. Such super-sensitive types are as easily upset in religious matters as in other spheres of life, on account of their peculiar ambivalent mentality. When someone sets a bad example, they follow it and throw the responsibility on the other.

Our patient, like other hysterics, is ambivalent in her attitude, not only towards God, Faith, and Church, but also towards the representative of the Church, the priest. The latter is especially apt to be the victim of ambivalent experiences for he represents a personality which embodies a very special interior conflict. In her dazed state, this attitude was revealed clearly. On the one hand, she wanted to be 'near to him in love'; and, on the other hand, in this very fashion to compromise and ruin him. There is another essential reason why priests, in particular, come to be entangled in such situations. We have already seen that the original object of these ambivalent attitudes is the *father*—the father to whom one would like to give oneself in love, but must not. The priest, as a celibate, occupies all too easily this very position, for in his case, too, the notion of sexual love is prohibited. He is thus an ideal subject for the transference of the interior conflict typifying the father-daughter situation. In passing, we might remark that here again we note the repetition of neurotic experience. Our case, in particular, presents us with another factor which seems to be of decisive significance in the selection of the priest as the subject of an imagined wish-fulfilment. The patient explained that, while in her befogged state, she had the sensation that she would very soon have a child. To this she added that it seemed to be as if the child had been conceived through the Holy Spirit.

The ambivalent patient, as we know, yearned on the one hand for sexual intercourse; but, on the other, felt a powerful inhibition, and it was this situation that impelled her to the notion of rape. In regard to the child, we find the same kind of ambivalent attitude: she wants a child, but as she does not want her husband as father she is faced with another inhibition, for it would be sinful to have another man as father. But in her imagination she finds a way out: 'Yes—a child, but the father is the Holy Spirit!' Now her wish is fulfilled and she is free from sin. We need hardly explain how easily such a condition of the imagination leads to the selection of a priest.

*   *   *   *   *

We trust that we have made it clear, in our study of this case, that hysteria is not a term of abuse—as is still thought in some quarters—but an *illness*. We hope the reader will now find it easier to understand the special religious problems of these types, and will have gained a clear realisation of the very real danger they provide for the priest. In the case just reviewed the priest made a grave mistake; he gave the patient, when she felt unwell, the opportunity of resting in his house; and, even worse, offered her a separate room. He thus provided all that was needed for the building up of a case against him. There were no witnesses, so at first sight things looked bad for him. Let this case serve as a warning of the great caution needed when hysteria is suspected. For the recognition of the illness, some experience and a knowledge of modern psychology is needful.

Before concluding this chapter a word as to the treatment of these cases. We have noticed that, more especially amongst priests, misleading ideas on this subject are common.

The reader has seen that a series of unsatisfied urges and wishes played a decisive part in bringing about the peculiar state of the patient. To prevent the recurrence of such pathological states, the buried material must be brought up from the subconscious into the conscious mind. We saw, for example, that the patient described her marriage as good, whereas in reality it was far from good; she cherished feelings of hatred towards her husband, due largely to her inferior position in the home. That has to be made clear to her conscious mind. The next step is to meet her difficulties and solve her problems, as far as is possible; not in a one-sided way —thinking of herself alone—but in a spirit of mutual understanding. She must have the courage to bring her conflicts out into the open and have a look at them. There must be no more evasion. This does *not* mean that she should give rein to her resentment against her husband and, possibly, look to divorce as a solution. To cling to the illusion that the marriage is good or to abandon it, are really one and the same thing, seen from different angles, for in both cases we have a neurotic escape mechanism. The same method holds good for all sexual problems met with in psychotherapy: the suppressed urges and tendencies must be brought out into daylight, into the world of the conscious mind. This does not mean, however, that now one can let go of the reins. To allow oneself to be dominated and guided by blind urges from the lower levels of the self is merely another kind of neurotic solution and one liable to make the neurosis worse. A thorough searching of the soul is the first step towards a real cure. Confession may have a valuable therapeutic influence. Then comes a knowledge of self. The next stage is a courageous facing of the problems, now that they are known and not hidden. This should be followed by their solution on positive lines.

We cannot conclude better than by telling the reader that our patient took the path we have recommended: she remade her marriage on a new and honourable foundation. Today she is a happy and satisfied mother.

CHAPTER VI

SOME PROBLEMS OF OBSESSIONAL NEUROSIS

As in the foregoing chapter, we cannot discuss all the problems raised by the theme. The best we can do is to make a selection of the most important, singling out those of special significance to the priest.

Every priest knows many of the faithful who, at least in outward appearance, give the greatest attention to their religious life. They are 'more Catholic than the Pope'; everywhere they dread sin, they are never fully satisfied with their self-examination, and always regard their repentance and their intentions as inadequate. They never cease to bring fresh charges against themselves; they feel they have forgotten something, search eagerly for sinful thoughts and are convinced that they have not made a full confession; while acts of penance are a source of fresh scruples. They are attacked by more fears in between confession and communion, and feel they have thought or done something sinful; at the same time they are not quite sure whether they did really sin or not, and dare not receive communion; then they make a fresh confession—often more than one—but without experiencing any change of feeling or improvement. Such people are hindered in their ordinary daily lives also by continual inhibitions of an obsessional nature, connected with religious ideas. These are the scruple-ridden, who convert their whole lives, including, of course, their religious practices, into prolonged ceremonial acts of an obsessional nature. This is obsessional neurosis invading the field of religion. (It should be mentioned in passing that obsessional symptoms can occur also in certain cases of insanity, more especially in melancholia; but in practice the neurotic cases are most likely to come within the scope of the priest). Important problems confront the priest in such cases. What exactly is obsessional neurosis? What is the connection between it and religion? Is this condition caused by religion? What is the inward nature of the disorder? What is its cause? How must a priest judge such people; and how can he help them?

1. *What is obsessional neurosis?* To use the words of H. Meng (*Das psychoanalytische Volksbuch*: Huber, Berne: 1939), it is, 'a painful state of anxiety causing the sufferer to feel a compulsion to think, speak, or do something or other, even though he is convinced that it is unpractical, senseless, impossible, or crazy——' We distinguish between obsessional ideas, obsessional impulses, obsessional actions, and obsessional inhibitions. If the patient seeks to evade the compulsion, to resist it, to refuse obedience, he finds he cannot do it—or not for long: in the end, *he has to give way*, otherwise he is overwhelmed by unbearable fear, although he does not know why or of what he is afraid. The sensation of fear does not pass away until the sufferer gives in to the compulsion. The sensation of fear and anxiety which accompanies the compulsion is due to a fear that he may be prevented from performing the task imposed by the disorder, or may be hindered in his fulfilment of the ritual demanded, so that he does not complete it. Everybody has, at one time or another, some symptoms of this kind: such as stepping on the paving stones according to some pattern, counting windows or steps, perhaps going back to see if the bath-tap was turned off, or some other little ritual. But there is a vast difference between such isolated tendencies and the fact of a definite, established neurosis of this sort. In the case of a true obsessional neurosis, the acts performed under compulsion acquire the status of an essential ritual, repeated over and over again. This is an indication that it stands *in the place of something else*, of which it is a symbol, and thus *cannot* be abandoned without producing unbearable sensations of fear.

This type of neurosis often begins to be manifest in childhood, as we shall see later. It sometimes runs a peculiar course. After periods of intense brooding, which may go on for hours or even days, or after the performance of lengthy ritualistic acts, the obsessional impulse seems exhausted for a time; but it can always break out again if some event releases it. Many patients know what is liable to bring about a new attack and seek to avoid the occasion—when the avoidance creates a new ceremonial of its own. It is obvious that the symptomatology of a serious neurosis of this kind must lead to an appalling limitation of personality and of its possibilities. Inhibitions hedge the patient on every side, and almost everything is connected with some notion of fear and anxiety. The patient will avoid many spheres of life altogether because he dreads to enter them. The consequence may be that all enjoyment of life vanishes and, in some cases, the patient entertains thoughts of suicide, which may themselves have a compulsory character. It is easy to imagine how tormenting such a state can be: it is made worse by the fact that the sufferer knows quite well that he is being driven to things that are senseless and yet he has to do them. He is aware of his own condition. P. Federn speaks of 'the forced labour' to which these unfortunate people are condemned. Fortunately, in some of these cases, the severest symptoms have a way of disappearing for a period even without any treatment.

2. *The nature and cause of obsessional neurosis, and its connection with religion.* The priest will naturally come into contact mainly with cases of a religious nature. At the same time, we need hardly say that there are many of these neurotics whose ritualistic acts have nothing to do with religious ideas or customs. It has been asserted frequently by opponents of religion that religion is the cause of obsessional neurosis: the strictness of the commandments turns men into obsessional neurotics. There is a very simple answer to this: namely that this type of neurosis is found quite frequently amongst non-religious individuals. It may, however, be true that in carrying out certain religious acts—such as in the confessional—obsessional symptoms are more than usually apt to manifest themselves. It will be shown later why this is so.

At this stage, we can only say that this connection is not conditioned by religion but by *the particular character of the disorder*; it cannot, accordingly, be said that confession for example, causes the disorder. In what direction the peculiar symptoms of this kind of neurosis will break out will depend upon the possibilities which offer themselves. The fact of religious rituals conditioned by neurosis means simply that the disorder is finding expression in this field. It can express itself, as we have remarked, in any field; with religious people it is, of course, likely to find its way into religious customs. Obsessional neurosis may frequently find an outlet in this field, but it is not itself conditioned by religion. Many patients, as a means of overcoming their anxieties, seek out a species of ceremony or ritual of a particularly complex kind. In this search, many discover religion which, with its rigid commandments, seems to offer numerous opportunities for expressing neurotic desires for ritual observance. In an earlier work, we drew attention to the fact that this goes so far that even completely non-religious people use religious forms as a framework on which to hang their own morbid ritualism, without acquiring even the slightest inward relationship to religion. The reader will recollect that we have spoken of the abuse of religious forms by neurotic cases. Recently, a sufferer from this type of neurosis who was wholly devoid of religious faith confirmed our views in a striking manner. She said: 'If there were no laws and commandments of the Church I should really have to invent them, for they give me a perfect means for releasing my compulsory urges.' G. Jud has pointed out that many persons become neurotic, 'because they make use of religion as a screen behind which they carry out, in forbidden fashion, a deformation of their own nature.' In cases of obsessional neurosis, the abuse of religion in this deformation takes place along somewhat different lines. The religious element in a compulsory neurosis is nothing other than a symptom of a psychic disorder manifesting itself in the field of religion. We shall show later, however, that this does not cover the entire field of the problems raised.

We now come to the question of *causes*. There is an outstanding fact which must at once strike us, when we begin to investigate the causes of these distressing states; and this should serve as a signpost. Is it not remarkable that such powerful sensations of fear and anxiety should be attached to such apparently unimportant matters? When a patient suffers from a continual fear that he may utter a certain word of no significance, perhaps inadvertently, this discrepancy becomes glaringly manifest. So much care is worthy of a better object. For this reason, Freud speaks of the *mesalliance* between the notion in the patient's mind and the manner in which it affects him. It is this crass discrepancy which put him on the right track, in his exploration of the mystery of this disease. The layman would say the effect was out of all proportion to the cause, that it was totally exaggerated, and the conclusion drawn by the patient that he has committed a criminal act—for example in uttering the forbidden word—is wrong. But the doctor will say, No *the effect is justified*, there is nothing wrong with the feeling of guilt suffered by the patient; but it should be attached to *another* cause and not to the notion of the patient. This true cause is unknown and must be dug up out of the sub-conscious mind. The notion in the patient's mind has mistakenly become attached to powerful emotional reactions. We are not accustomed to have reactions of this sort in the absence of some idea in the mind to account for them: therefore, when this idea is lacking, we adopt some other, which seems suitable, much as the police, when they cannot find the real criminal, arrest someone else in his place. The fact of the false attachment explains in itself the impotence of reason to resist the painful idea.

When Freud became convinced that the compulsory acts of the patient must be related to motives quite different from those supposed by the patient, he set to work to discover the *real* motives lying behind the symptoms, and through a careful analysis of numerous cases he succeeded in doing this.

He came to the following conclusions. Each compulsion takes

the place of an earlier urge which, for some reason, has been suppressed and thrust down into the subconscious—most often because it is an urge not tolerated by our moral standards. These urges are, so to say, underground *wishes*, which conscience causes us to reject. In the compulsory symptoms, these wishes find a substitute satisfaction, whereby at the same time the patient's feeling of guilt expresses itself in the tormenting nature of the disease. The patient is, of course, wholly unaware of his guilt and of its cause. For the sense of guilt is no longer attached to its original cause: it exists in an isolated state and in the absence of its true object it has to look for a substitute, upon which it can release itself. This it finds in the compulsory mechanism of the illness. As a result of this double transposition, the patient fails to realise the actual meaning of his feelings of compulsion. The compulsory symptom may indicate the true cause, without the patient being able to understand.

*   *   *   *   *

We will now illustrate the cure of a neurosis of this sort by describing a particular case. A young girl became ill, suffering from violent obsessional notions. She felt an inward compulsion to imagine all sorts of sexual things; she was especially tormented by the idea that she *must* have sexual intercourse with her brother. Actually, her life as regards sexual matters, was beyond reproach. In consequence of her neurosis, she presented a very difficult problem to the priest: she went to confession many times a day, every day of the week; she felt she had to obtain absolution whenever the thoughts which troubled her returned, although she did not experience the relief she hoped for in this way. She never received communion, because the thoughts always came back and convinced her she was unworthy.

In the first session of her analysis, the patient related two dreams which led to an explanation of her trouble.

In the first dream, she said, she is sitting near to her father in his office and acting as his secretary. Other employees are also present. I call to my father: 'Papa, please send all the others away; I want to be your only employee.' The second dream dealt with her brother: he is very ill, she is nursing him and sits by the bed. Suddenly he falls over and dies. She tells her mother and both of them cry. After relating this dream, she explained that almost every night she dreamed of her brother's death.

It is easy to see that these dreams are linked together by a common factor. The patient desires to be the only child of her father. At first she *was* an only child; then the brother came and thrust her aside. The consequence was a hatred strong enough to cause a death-wish. This wish she felt to be sinful and accordingly thrust it down into her subconscious. To the subconscious mind, however, a wish is the same thing as a deed. Her obsessional notions are a substitute for the satisfaction of the repressed urge, and the torments she suffers through her symptoms are a punishment which her sense of guilt drives her to inflict upon herself —although she is not aware of the forbidden urge nor does she know why she feels guilty. But the unceasing repetition of the compulsory idea of intercourse with her brother can be taken as a symbolic indication of where the real cause is to be sought.

We have now seen that the emotional reactions of the patient are linked with a false occasion. There has been a transposition, and only by means of psychotherapeutic treatment can we discover the true links. Freud laid great stress on the fact that one cannot truly understand these compulsive cases until one has seen through their pseudo-morality. He tells us of an official who suffered from innumerable doubts and scruples. Freud was struck by his odd behaviour in always handing him brand new bank notes in payment after a consultation. He made a special point of not passing on dirty paper money as he was afraid it might carry dangerous germs, capable of causing grave injury to the recipient. At that time, Freud had already a vague premonition of a connection between neurosis and sexual life, and he ventured to ask the patient,

on another occasion, some questions as to his sex life: 'Oh, everything is all right,' he said, 'in that direction I have all that I need:
I know several good families in whose homes I play the part of
the nice old uncle; and this enables me, now and then, to invite
a young girl for an excursion in the country. I then arrange things
so that we miss the last train home and are compelled to spend
the night in some inn, where I take two rooms—I do things in
proper style, you know—and later, when the girl has retired, I
pay a visit to her room.' 'But are you not afraid that you will
cause harm to the girl?' asked Freud. The patient burst out angrily:
'Harm? what would harm her? I never harmed a girl and no
girl ever objected.' He was so much offended that he left the room
and never came back.

Freud, commenting on this case, says that he could explain the
contrast between his patient's ultra-conscientious attitude in
the matter of the money, and the striking absence of conscience
in the way he took advantage of girls entrusted to his care, in no
other way than by assuming a transposition of his sense of guilt.
If he had placed his scruples where they belonged, he would have
had to give up his sexual adventures, with the satisfaction they
gave him. As it was, it is clear that he achieved by the transposition
and illness a gain that was important to him.

In like manner, our girl patient evaded her real problem by a
displacement. Instead of facing the real problem of her wrong
attitude towards her brother, she developed a compulsory neurosis
of a sexual nature, although her sex life was not open to objection
and gave no ground for scruples, as she knew very well deep
down in herself. It is clear that a difference exists between this case
of ours and the case cited by Freud of the official who had a complex
about paper money. In the case of the girl, there was a feeling of
guilt resulting from sensations thrust down into the subconscious;
there was no *real* sin, for there was no conscious consent. In the
case given by Freud, the feeling of guilt arose from repeated
real acts of a sinful nature: the disorder was not the feeling of sin

—which was justified—but the manner in which it manifested itself.

Thus we perceive, in these cases, *two* tendencies for the discovery of which we are indebted to psycho-analysis of the Freudian school. On the one hand, a quite morbid willingness to endure suffering; on the other, an exaggerated tendency towards freedom on the instinctive level. Now, one takes the lead, now the other, and each is conditioned by the other. The attitude of the sufferer towards conscience is markedly ambivalent. He endeavours, with passionate intensity, to fulfil the claims of his conscience; but at the same time, he seeks to make a fool of conscience. We may claim to have demonstrated, along these lines, that the assertion —not infrequently heard—that psycho-analysis seeks to make men 'amoral' is quite devoid of foundation, if its teaching is rightly understood and applied. On the contrary, it aims at bringing amoral tendencies, which have been suppressed, up to the level of consciousness, so that they can be faced and conquered.

*   *   *   *   *

3. *What should be the attitude of the priest towards these cases; and how can he help them?*

A. In the first place, the priest must be in a position to know a victim of obsessional neurosis of the religious type when he meets with one. This is usually not difficult. It is to be noted that the victim is never *fundamentally* convinced as to the forgiveness of sins; this is one of the most significant indications. The reader will understand from the foregoing material why this must be the case.

B. In the religious field, the priest may make certain mistakes. We know that these cases follow a special pattern; they present the appearance of being excessively religious. The priest has to be very careful not to be taken in by this; he must not co-operate with the patient in his neurotic behaviour, and, above all, he must not encourage his symptoms, thus acquiescing in his misuse of religion as a means of satisfying his disordered mind. The priest must never forget that, while the subject *seems* to be troubled with religious conflicts, his real trouble is a psychic disorder. This illness cannot possibly be 'absolved away,' as J. Miller neatly puts it, and this must be realised clearly. Accordingly the priest's first concern should be to place the sufferer under psychotherapeutic treatment. In these cases, particularly, it is highly important that the treatment should begin in good time. It would be idle to pretend that obsessional neurosis is not a very serious therapeutic problem; in more advanced cases, the prognosis is unfavourable.

The priest is often the first to have an opportunity of diagnosing a disorder which frequently reveals itself for the first time in the confessional. We should like to draw special attention to the fact that, even as early as the first confession, compulsory mechanisms may be manifested. We have been told by a number of patients suffering from compulsory neurosis in so severe a form as to be practically beyond treatment, that they first noticed the symptoms of their neurosis at the time of their first confession. If, at this time, treatment had been commenced, the later distressing developments of the disease might well have been prevented. On the matter of the relationship between confession and neurosis, we would like to remark that the statement—made at a much later date—that the symptoms began with the first confession, is certainly not wholly in keeping with the facts; we are compelled to believe that such symptoms manifested themselves in one way or another, earlier on in childhood. These other occasions were less striking and thus passed into oblivion, while the great event of the first confession—an occasion remembered for a lifetime— remained permanently linked in the mind with the neurotic symptoms then noticed. The reader of this study will not find it difficult to understand that confession is, in general, an institution in connection with which the compulsory mechanisms of this type of neurosis are very likely to manifest themselves. We have already described an *ambivalent attitude towards conscience* as an essential characteristic of obsessional neurotics; and it is obvious that this ambivalence will come to light when the conscience is probed.

C. We hope that the final conclusions to be drawn from the foregoing are now clear. In obsessional neurosis we have to do with a disorder which, on medical and spiritual grounds, should receive appropriate therapeutic treatment as soon as possible. As a proof of this, it is sufficient to point out that neurotics of this type will not seldom acquire an attitude of resentment against the sacrament of absolution because (as they say), 'it doesn't work' in their cases. Such patients must be given to understand clearly that *they are ill* and need, in the first place, a cure on the natural level. We have stressed the fact that this kind of neurosis is conditioned by feelings of guilt and that the discovery of these must precede a cure. This process in itself has nothing to do with the cure, unless, through the analysis, a genuine guilt, requiring forgiveness, comes to light. We wish to warn priests most emphatically against themselves discovering the above described mechanism of guilt transference in these cases: the result of such action would be to bring about a worsening of the patient's state, leading possibly to utter despair. The task of the priest is to promote treatment through a competent psychotherapist, at the earliest opportunity, while himself guaranteeing right religious guidance. Further, he must know that no guilt attaches to the compulsion as such in the case of obsessional neurotics. After treatment, a new situation may arise under certain conditions. It is a question of whether the symptoms of obsession take the place of tendencies thrust down into the subconscious, which do not represent any real guilt from a moral-theological viewpoint, as with our girl patient, or whether they stand for a real guilt persistently carried on, or only very partially suppressed, as with the case cited by Freud. All this can be made clear only after a thorough analytical treatment. In the first case, actual sin could result only if the patient, after being conscious of the forbidden tendency and being cured of the neurosis, gave a voluntary assent to the evil tendency. In the second case, it is manifest that real sin exists and calls for forgiveness. Speaking generally, the path to be followed passes through the following stages: discovery of the more or less suppressed forbidden (or felt to be forbidden) wishes, the overcoming of these, the abandonment of satisfaction or substitute satisfaction, cure on the natural level, knowledge and confession of all sins, repentance for having sinned against God in as far as it took place with conscious assent, a firm resolution not to sin again, and absolution—in fact a cure on the religious side.

The placing of sufferers from obsessional and other forms of neurosis in the hands of a psychotherapist should therefore be insisted upon, not only on the grounds of general humanity, but as a *necessary* act from the standpoint of the care of souls. It is often therapy which first makes it possible for the patient to distinguish clearly between mechanisms of a diseased form in the psychic field, and religious life; and it often enables him to understand in what fashion he has previously—despite being highly conscientious—deceived his own conscience and what advantages he thus obtained. The aim in view must be that a dynamic process in the field of religion should take the place of the previous fixation on wrong lines. The further development of this process will depend upon free personal decision and the grace of God.